OIL
IN TROUBLED
WATERS

OIL
IN TROUBLED
WATERS

Madelyn Klein Anderson

THE VANGUARD PRESS, INC.

NEW YORK

Library of Congress Cataloging in Publication Data

Anderson, Madelyn Klein.
Oil in troubled waters.

Includes index.
SUMMARY: Discusses how oil seeps into the world's
waters, the methods used to clean up such spills,
and possible ways to prevent spills of varying size.
1. Oil spills—Environmental aspects. [1. Oil
spills—Environmental aspects. 2. Oil pollution of
rivers, harbors, etc.] I. Title.
TD427.P4A52   628.1'6833   80-21139
ISBN 0-8149-0842-X

Designer: Tom Bevans
Manufactured in the United States of America.

1   2   3   4   5   6   7   8   9   0

To Justin:
messenger, escort — and champion

ACKNOWLEDGMENTS

Many people in many organizations have provided invaluable material for this book: the United States Coast Guard; the United States Navy; the Environmental Protection Agency at Edison, N.J.; the National Wildlife Federation; the Oil Spill Engineer of the New York State Department of Transportation; the New York Zoological Society (Bronx Zoo); the American Petroleum Institute; and Shel Holtz of ARCO, American Richfield Company. Thank you. Thanks also to Bernice Woll for her perceptive editing, Bill Jaber for reading manuscript, Karin Mango for indexing, and to the dozens of friends and acquaintances who provided an extensive clipping service.

CONTENTS

IRELAND

WALES

Milford Haven •

CORNWALL

GREAT BRITAIN

Seven Stones

Land's End

SCILLY ISLES

Where Torrey Canyon ran aground

English Channel

ATLANTIC OCEAN

BRITTANY

FRANCE

CHAPTER

1

Shipwreck

Some fifteen miles west of Land's End, the tip of Britain's foot in the sea, stand the Seven Stones — barely awash at high tide, poking out of the water at low tide. Like the toes of some mischievous sea monster playing with the water, they lie in wait beside one of the most heavily traveled sea routes in the world and have caught many a storm-driven sailing ship. Today's ships, of course, are not the pawns of wind and weather that their forebears were; however, with the help of a lightship, they still keep a respectful distance from the treacherous Stones.

But on a Saturday morning in March 1967, a huge ship, a tanker, made directly for the Stones. Frantic signals from the lightship went unheeded, apparently unseen. The ship was the *Torrey Canyon*, then one of the largest in the world. Carrying over 29 million gallons of crude oil from the Persian Gulf, she had rounded the Cape of Good Hope, sailed up the western coast of Africa, passed the coasts of Spain and France, and now she was only a few hours from her destination, the giant port at Milford Haven in Wales. Straining every resource, she was hurrying to make the late evening tide in. Missing that high tide would mean waiting five expensive, tedious days for another tide high enough to float her heavy load. To save a precious half-hour, the *Torrey Canyon* took a shortcut that could bring her close to the Seven Stones.

Aware of the danger in his maneuver, Captain Pastrenzo Rugiati took the wheel himself to make the necessary course change. That accomplished, he locked the controls into their automatic setting, and walked away. Glancing around to make a quick check of the ship's position, he saw — with sickening clarity — that he had miscalculated the degree of turn necessary to skirt the Stones. His ship was closing rapidly on the treacherous toes. He shouted for a "hard left!" A crewman sprang to the wheel, then called out in alarm when the wheel would not turn. The captain, realizing instantly that the crewman had not disengaged the automatic control, flung himself at the wheel and fought to clear the Seven Stones. Too late. The highest, Pollard Rock, caught the *Torrey Canyon*, ripped open her hull, and held her fast.

Oil streamed out of the *Torrey Canyon*'s cargo tanks. The crew, unharmed, worked feverishly to refloat the ship, pumping out still more of her cargo to lighten her. Help summoned by radio and the lightship was quick to come and grew in volume as the extent of the problem was realized.

Experts consulted on the massive problem of refloating the tanker. Holes were plugged, air was pumped into cargo tanks. The salvage operations were dangerous — oil mixed with air gives off gases so vola-

The *Torrey Canyon*, broken and awash. Part of Pollard Rock is just visible in the center of the picture.

tile that the static electricity generated by a nylon shirt can explode them. Aboard the *Torrey Canyon* were a lot more sparks than that — from welding torches, from electric pumps offloading cargo, and from emergency generators providing the light by which to work.

Then danger turned into disaster: Captain Hans Barend, chief of salvage operations, opened the door to the engine room, and that simple act caused an explosion so violent that the Captain was thrown overboard and killed. Eight others were injured.

The explosion caused a small fire, but the heavy oil was not very flammable and the tanker did not go up in flames. Then gale-force winds came up, pounding the *Torrey Canyon* against the Stones. Her hull torn, her structure weakened by days of constant pulling and

11

pushing by the tides, the *Torrey Canyon* finally broke in two. Thirty thousand tons of oil came pouring out. Worse, fifty thousand tons more remained inside the wreck, leaking out slowly, constantly — a source of contamination for years to come if something were not done. It was decided to bomb the wreck to release the oil so that the oxygen in the atmosphere would allow it to be burned off. But it took three days of bombing with napalm and high explosives before the burn-off was accomplished.

In the meanwhile, the oil that had once been part of the *Torrey Canyon*'s cargo was well on its way eastward to the shores of Great Britain, heading for the lovely beaches and rocky foreshores of Cornwall.

A panicky government dug up a report on an experiment done years before showing that *detergents*, chemical cleaning agents, break up the molecules of oil. It seemed the most effective method of cleanup. Factories went on 24-hour emergency shifts to make the detergent. The Royal Navy went into action, spraying the detergents on the slick. The spraying equipment worked poorly, so the men resorted to emptying the drums of detergents overboard, mixing the chemicals into the oil with the ship's propellers. For days, thirty to seventy thousand gallons of detergents were poured into the oil.

Instead of the oil breaking up, however, the oil-water-detergent mixture turned into a gooey mess that seemed to grow like magic. The mix looked like creamy chocolate fudge or pudding, and was promptly dubbed "mousse," to the everlasting disgust of gourmet fans of that delicate dessert. Slabs of the stuff two feet thick lay on beaches and rocks. Worse, the detergents were adding to the death toll among the birds — wherever the mousse touched, it burned. Nor were human beings immune to the caustic detergents. Gloves, hoods, smocks, and goggles were flown in to protect the workers. There was no protection, however, against the nauseating odor that made many of them throw up.

An army of volunteers pitched in to help the military. Firemen hosed, gardeners sprinkled, construction workers bulldozed. Beauticians even used their sinks and hair dryers to clean oiled sea birds. Everybody dug and shoveled and scraped.

The supply of cleaning rags ran out. An urgent appeal over radio, television, and in newspapers soon brought donations of rags from all over the world.

Tons of small fish were brought in to feed the thousands of oiled birds rounded up from the rocks and shallows and housed in hastily set-up treatment centers. But where do you store all that fish? More urgent calls for help — until a London hotelkeeper suggested a refrigerated boxcar, quickly donated.

Still, the massive, dirty, stinking job was getting out of hand. As the oil touched down sometimes here, sometimes there, people and cleaning equipment had to be moved to where they were most needed, causing tremendous problems of transportation and housing.

Finally, about a month after the wreck of the *Torrey Canyon*, the worst seemed to be over. It was — in Great Britain. But in France the fight against the odorous black tide was just beginning, as the oil swept onto the shores of Brittany. This landfall caught the French by surprise. They had expected it farther south, and valuable time was lost in getting workers and equipment to the spill.

France fought the oil differently from Great Britain. Dismayed by the detergents' damage to wildlife and the difficulties of cleaning up the mousse, France decided to soak up the oil instead, using sawdust, volcanic ash, and leather shavings. The plan was to then burn the oiled debris. But the mess, heavily mixed with water, refused to burn. So soldiers, sailors, and civilians — firemen, police, and other volunteers, including school children — shoveled the stuff into buckets, emptied the buckets into trucks, and trucked it to burial sites. The buried oil started seeping into surrounding farmlands, ruining crops. France's cleanup wasn't working any better than Britain's.

The largest bird sanctuary in Europe, Brittany's Sept Iles (Seven Isles), had suffered severe damage. Hundreds of thousands of sea birds were dead. Valuable oyster and mussel beds were ruined. Fish tasted of oil and no one would eat them. Farmers feared for their crops, fishermen for their catches, consumers for their health. Business people who depend on tourists coming to their beaches were faced with thousands of canceled reservations. . . . The financial losses from the *Torrey Canyon* spill threatened to last for years. Above all was the appalling ugliness and the spoilage of nature's limited resources.

And the oil from the *Torrey Canyon* moved with winds and currents to the shores of Holland and Spain.

The oil from *one* wrecked tanker was doing all this. *Thousands* of these tankers rode the seas, and their cargoes were absolutely essential to keep the world running, to power and lubricate machinery and automotive engines, to heat homes and factories, to make medicines and countless other products.

The world worried, and governments moved to control and clean the oil from our waters.

For eleven years the 119,000-ton spill from the *Torrey Canyon* was to be the world's largest. Then, on March 16, 1978, just two days short of the anniversary of the *Torrey Canyon* disaster, the supertanker *Amoco Cadiz*, moved up the coast of Britanny, suffered a power failure that caused her to lose steering. A call for assistance brought a tug to her side, but as the two captains argued over salvage shares, the *Amoco Cadiz* drifted onto some offshore rocks. A myriad of small tankers and tugs negotiated the dangerous rocks in the attempt to offload cargo and refloat the supertanker. But towlines snapped and hoses could not be connected — the seas were too high, the *Amoco Cadiz* too big. Large as she was, however, she could not withstand the forces of nature. Gale winds and waves pounding her on the rocks finally opened her to the sea. Some 220,000 tons of oil came pouring out.

Again the French were faced with massive cleanup problems. Divers attached explosives to the hull of the *Amoco Cadiz* to force out remaining pockets of oil, to prevent months of continuous seepage. They turned to the use of detergents for the cleanup in deep water, but, as with the *Torrey Canyon*, their major thrust was with special absorbents like chalk and shredded paper. Over 5,000 military and civilians struggled with the mess. They scraped and shoveled and pumped. They dug ditches above the high-water line to receive

15

oil-soaked debris. Their eyes and throats were irritated, they suffered from diarrhea, dizziness, chest pains, and nausea. Shellfish died, birds died, the fishing and tourist industries suffered. . . .

Little had changed in the eleven years since the *Torrey Canyon* spill, except that this one was twice as big.

The *Amoco Cadiz* did not hold its record for long, however. On June 3, 1978, a Mexican offshore oil well blew out in Campeche Bay in the Gulf of Mexico, some 500 miles south of Texas. *Blowout preventers*, safety devices meant to clamp off a wild flow, had failed to engage properly.

For almost ten months the well, Ixtoc I, spewed hundreds of thousands of gallons of oil from a wellhead eighty feet below the surface of the water. Teams of specialists in fighting wild wells, including one headed by the world-famous Red Adair, failed in many attempts to stop the deluge. A huge steel bell nicknamed a "sombrero" was designed to cap the flow of oil, gas, and water so they could be separated, the oil going to storage, the gas allowed to escape, the water sent back to the sea. However, the sombrero did not perform as well as had been hoped. A relief well was drilled at an angle to Ixtoc I in the hope of drawing off the explosive pressure in the wild well. It failed. Then thousands of two-inch steel and lead balls and canvas patches were injected through the relief well into Ixtoc I. These slowed the rate of spill, as did a second relief well, finished in December of 1979. But it was not until March 24, 1980, that Ixtoc I was stopped, capped with cement plugs. Estimates of the final total of oil spilled vary widely — any-

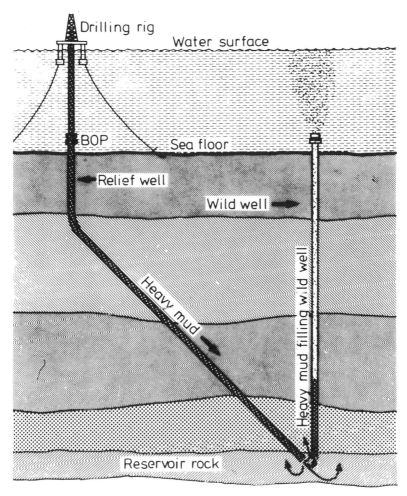

Drilling rig
Water surface
BOP
Sea floor
Relief well
Wild well
Heavy mud
Heavy mud filling wild well
Reservoir rock

One method of drilling a relief well.
(BOP stands for "breakout preventer.")

where from about 717,000 tons to three or four times that amount.

Remarkably, and fortunately, little of the oil washed up on Texas and Mexican shorelines. Favorable winds and currents kept much of the oil away from the

Texas coast, moving it back and forth in the Gulf. But as tides shift the threat of contamination will be present for years. The full environmental impact, particularly in Mexico, where officials seem reluctant to release statistics, may never be learned.

The world still worries about the cost of spilled oil to the environment and to life itself, both human and animal. To that concern is added still another — for the oil itself. We can ill afford to lose the precious petroleum that keeps our world functioning.

2

Precious Oils

Oils — of the olive, the nut, the fish, the whale — have been part of the sea trade since human beings first ventured forth in frail boats to barter and buy. And oil has spilled from boats for all those many thousands and thousands of years.

Once of these early seafarers, probably carrying oil in clay containers, might have had to toss his cargo overboard to lighten his load, much as the *Torrey Canyon* and *Amoco Cadiz* had to do. Or perhaps a container of oil washed overboard in a storm and its contents spilled. The traders probably watched in amazement as the oil calmed the angry sea around their boats. And, indeed, a few quarts of vegetable or fish oil poured slowly onto swells will calm thousands of square feet of water. (No one knows for sure if the oil actually squashes the angry whitecaps or whether the oil makes the foaming bubbles break faster — so fast that, like the moving blades of a fan, they become invisible.) Whatever the reason, "pouring oil on troubled waters" calms them, and the phrase has become a cliché for making peace among people as well as on the water.

A tanker under tow, broken in half and spilling a great volume of oil—the light patches. (Note the difference in the swells between the slicks and the open water.)

PRECIOUS OILS

Although a little fish or vegetable oil may calm troubled waters, the fossil oil called *petroleum* has certainly ruffled them — and us. Petroleum comes from accumulations of *fossils* — plant and animal life (particularly seaweeds, mollusks, and microscopic animals) buried under the pressure of water, earth, and rocks for thousands of years. Over many centuries some buried fossils changed into chemical compounds of hydrogen and carbon — *hydrocarbons* — that we now call petroleum. Depending on where they were buried and their chemical transformation, other fossilized material changed into natural gas and coal. The three — coal, natural gas, and petroleum — are called *fossil fuels* because of their origin. Petroleum, particularly asphalt, and coal are also known as *bitumens* because of their chemical compositions.

Petroleum is found in rocks of every geological age in the Earth's crust and is widely distributed around the world. Depending on their location, the types of petroleum and their chemical composition and appearance vary. Petroleum takes three forms: *crude oil*, a black, brown, greenish, or colorless liquid; *asphalt*, a near-solid; and *natural gas*. Petroleum's natural gas is something of a puzzle, since natural gas is also found where there are no signs of petroleum.

Petroleum has been known to human beings since the early days of history when small amounts were scooped up from shallow pools and pits. It was used for waterproofing dwellings and boats, and firebombing enemies in war. Babylonians paved their streets with it, and the Egyptians used it to grease the axles of their chariots. The Persians ate bitumens as medicine, and

21

when they conquered Egypt in 525 BC they broke up the mummies they found, thinking they were covered by bitumen. In some rare instances in ancient times, petroleum was even used for lighting. In more modern times, the city of Prague had several streets lit by petroleum lamps by 1815. The Indians of North America used petroleum for making "magic" and for paints and medicines. Explorers and wagon train settlers learned of these cures and eagerly traded for them. Peddlers bottled the petroleum and sold it as Seneca Oil or Genesee Oil, "good for everything that ails you and your horse and wagon, too."

Of course, supplies of petroleum in those days were limited to what could be found on the surface, although the Chinese had been drawing up oil with long bamboo tubes for some 4,000 years; and in the mid-1800s in Europe small amounts of petroleum had been extracted from *shale*, rock formed in layers from mud and clay. Then in 1859 a well was dug in a place now called Titusville, in Pennsylvania, a well that could bring oil from beneath the ground like water. And the world was never the same again.

Virtually concurrent with the newly available supply of petroleum was the capability of distilling it into a number of different products. Petroleum, like other liquids, is distilled by boiling, then capturing the vapor or steam that is emitted and condensing that vapor back into a liquid or a semi-solid that is physically different from the original liquid. Petroleum can be distilled at successively higher temperatures, each resulting in different end products called *fractions*, leaving behind *residual oils* that are refined in ways

The first oil well. The developer, Edwin Drake, is on the right.

other than by distilling. The fractions obtained by distilling petroleum are kerosene, naphtha, benzene, and gasoline. Particular petroleums yield varying amounts of heavier, more condensed fractions — fuel oils, lubricating oils, petrolatum (we know it as petroleum jelly or Vaseline), and paraffin. The petroleums of Pennsylvania, for instance, are particularly rich in paraffin.

Paraffin and kerosene were the major distillates in the early days of the oil industry. The paraffin soon replaced spermaceti for candles and the kerosene replaced whale oil in stoves and lamps. The search for the elusive whale was increasingly difficult and expensive, the whaling voyages more prolonged — but petroleum was coming out of the ground as fast as men could dig wells.

And what of that petroleum distillate known as gasoline? Well, they tried that, too, in stoves and lamps, but it exploded — so most of it was dumped. But the existence of gasoline soon made possible the development of a gasoline-driven engine — giving birth to the automobile, the tractor, the truck, the airplane.

Within less than 50 years that Titusville oil well had revolutionized the world, made it great, made it efficient, and made it dependent and thirsty for oil.

To satisfy that thirst, to produce more gasoline, scientists developed means other than steam distillation to break down petroleum into its fractions. These are mechanical, electrical, and chemical processes and are called *cracking.* It was a short step for scientists to turn the waste gases of the cracking processes into useful products. Among the chemical compounds they developed are alcohols, ethylene, propylene, acetylene, acetone, acetic acid, and ammonia. The scientists also developed petroleum-based materials like synthetic rubber, polystyrene, and polypropylene; and agricultural fertilizers and explosives.

Science made petroleum the keystone of any number of new industries and vital to the military defense of the country — over 60 percent of our tonnage overseas during World War II consisted of petroleum and petroleum products. We move on petroleum. We cool and heat our world with petroleum. At present, we cannot survive without petroleum.

24

As our usage increased astronomically, our supplies of petroleum dwindled. We turned to foreign sources of supply: petroleum is produced in the Soviet Union, Rumania, Iran, Kuwait, Libya, Iraq, Saudi Arabia, Algeria, West Africa, Venezuela, Mexico, West Canada, and Vietnam. We are now exploring the ocean bottoms, searching for the rich beds of petroleum buried there. We are also turning to experimental research on extracting oil from shale and from sand and we are looking desperately for petroleum substitutes — in the sun, in the wind, in the atom. . . .

Yet we remain dependent on foreign sources of oil, especially for particular types of petroleum. We find ourselves squeezed into political alliances and compromises with which we are not always comfortable. Indeed, we are finding ourselves less in partnership and more at the mercy of various suppliers, particularly the Arab countries, whose increasing oil prices and money manipulations have forced us into a series of economic crises. We have also suffered social turmoil as heads of government failed to lay an embargo on oil-rich Iran despite that country's taking of United States hostages. And how much of the Vietnam war was related to United States and Soviet desire to protect petroleum sources?

We suffer, too, internal crises among the Aleuts and Eskimos in Alaska, whose economy today depends on the oil industry, but whose society traditionally rests on hunting. They fear that increased offshore drilling for oil will endanger the seals and whales they hunt and eat. They fear government and corporate controls over their lands. But they desire the standard of living the oil and pipeline industry will give them.

25

We do not wish to spoil our environment, but we need petroleum — we need to be energy self-sufficient. For that new sources of petroleum must be found. Shale rock must be excavated, oceans must be explored by monstrous and potentially dangerous drilling rigs, some of the unspoiled reaches of the Alaskan wilds must be spoiled by a pipeline industry. Petroleum substitutes are not yet feasible alternatives and may never be; nor are wind, thermal, solar, or atomic sources of energy yet available in the amounts we need.

Good conservation practices are reducing that need, but we still need. Sometimes we must pay with uncomfortable compromises. The cost is high — too high to waste our supplies, to spill our oil.

3

Oil in the Rain . . . and Other Places

A little over six million tons of oil enter the oceans every year, says the National Academy of Sciences. Contrary to what you probably think, most of this oil does *not* come from tanker and offshore oil-well accidents, despite the amount of publicity given even the smallest of these spills. Spills account for only a very small amount of the oil in our waters.

Where, then, *does* the oil come from?

• You may find this hard to believe, but a great deal comes from people like you and me. We spill oil in our driveways, our gas stations, our streets. The service attendant empties old crankcase oil down a drain; you oil the gears on your bike; your car leaks oil. Machinery drips, pipes leak, storage tanks seep. One small oil terminal in New York City has been leaking since it was built — 100 years ago. Drips, leaks, and seeps get flushed by faucets and hoses and rainstorms into drains and sewers to reach lakes and rivers and oceans. One-fourth of the oil in our oceans come from these sources.

• One-tenth more of that estimated six million tons a year comes from another amazing source: the skies. Hydrocarbons are released from automobile and truck exhausts, from furnaces and machinery. The hydrocarbons reach the clouds, the clouds are moved by the winds, and some 600,000 tons of hydrocarbons fall with the rain and the snow into the oceans.

• Another 600,000 tons of oil in the water come from *beneath* the sea, from a source almost as old as the oceans themselves: natural seeps from petroleum beds still unfound, buried for millenia.

• A very small fraction of the National Academy's 600-million-ton figure comes from the rigs drilling into known beds of oil beneath the waters and from pipeline leaks. Of course, that fraction might be raised in a year with a major blowout such as the one in Campeche Bay. But blowouts are relatively rare — they just get a lot of publicity. However, as drilling increases in new areas of exploration — for example, in the Baltimore Canyon off the mid-Atlantic coast, the Beaufort Sea off Alaska, the Davis Straits between Canada and Greenland — and as new wells are brought in, their fractional contribution will increase, despite carefully planned deterrents. Rigs are growing increasingly complex and drilling is deeper and deeper. Some rigs are completely submerged and must function automatically. Underwater blowouts from such rigs would be exceedingly hard to stop should safety devices fail. In the frigid waters of the Arctic, blowouts would be impossible to stop.

• The National Academy of Science estimates that about one-third of the oil in the ocean comes from marine transportation. Only a tiny one-twentieth of that

A burning oil rig in the Gulf of Mexico. Coast Guard officers barely seen in the crow's nest (at top) search with binoculars to determine which of the rig's many wells is on fire. This fire took almost five months to extinguish.

amount comes from accidents. The rest — the giant portion — comes from routine spills by ships and boats.

Lightering, moving cargo from one ship to another, is a routine cause of spillage. The supertanker or VLCC (Very Large Crude Carrier), and the super-super-tanker or ULCC (Ultra Large Crude Carrier) are too big for most ports, so they must be lightered. These behemoths of the sea were developed when the Suez Canal was closed in the 1950s in a series of political-economic-military incidents among Egypt, Israel, Great Britain,

Ankle deep on the foam-covered deck of a tanker after it collided with a freighter, a Coast Guardsman plays a hose on blazing fuel oil at the mouth of the Mississippi.

and France. Tankers bringing oil from the rich fields of the Middle East could reach the Atlantic Ocean only by going the long way around South Africa's Cape of Good

Hope. To make this trip more economical, larger loads had to be carried on each voyage. The *Torrey Canyon*, for instance, was doubled in size by the insertion of an entire new midsection before its fatal voyage.

There are very few ports that can accomodate the supertanker. The United States, for instance, has only one superport in operation, and that is an offshore facility at Valdez, the southern terminus of the Alaskan Pipeline. Supertanker cargoes for the United States are unloaded at Caribbean ports connected to shore terminals by pipeline, or they are lightered into smaller ships or barges that *can* make port. Many of the small tankers used for lightering are worn-out, badly kept "rust buckets" with poorly trained crews. Opportunities for spills abound if transfer is handled carelessly or equipment breaks.

Cleaning out at sea causes a high percentage of the marine transportation figure. There are about 50,000 tankers and other merchant ships afloat, and millions of small pleasure boats — and all of them have to clean their *bilges*, the bottommost section, of the oily water that collects there. Merchant ships drydock at least once every 18 months, and they must be clean and gas-free when they do. About half of the merchant ships and the vast number of pleasure boats clean out at sea. Tankers also have to clear out their *ballast water*, water carried in their cargo tanks when they are not transporting oil to weight down the ship so that it rides more smoothly and is more maneuverable. When it is flushed out, ballast water carries *sludge*, the tarry residue of oil in the tanks from previous cargoes. Ports have the facilities to receive this waste, but not all ships bother using them.

31

These are deliberate spills, accounting for almost one-third of all the oil entering our waters annually. Such spills can be criminal: it is illegal for ships to wash out within 200 miles of the United States coastline.

More than 15,000 spills are reported every year in the United States. We cannot even begin to know how many are never reported, never discovered — and never even considered a spill by most of the public — the public that unwittingly spills millions of gallons of oil a year.

4

Oil and Water
and Life

What happens when oil spills into the water? What does oil do to the marine environment? What happens to the water, the fish, other animals and plants of the sea, and the tide pools and the marshes? To the sea birds? And what is the effect of oil in our waters on human beings, on you?

There aren't any pat answers to these questions. Nobody really asked them until the *Torrey Canyon* broke up on the Seven Stones. Indeed, some of the questions were asked only yesterday, as our awareness of the fallout from environmental pollution slowly grows.

We *have* learned that the truism "oil and water don't mix" is not completely true. Oil *does* separate out of water and, when the two are mixed, rises to the top. That's because oil is lighter than water. You can see this for yourself. Pour a tablespoon of cooking oil into a cup, then fill the cup with water. Does the oil float up, making a large circle on top of the water? You've made an oil slick. Now stir the slick into the water and wait a minute. You will see most of the oil come to the surface again. *Most*, but not all. Some of the water has entered a few of the molecules of oil, and this oil has therefore become heavier. The heavier oil is unable to rise to the surface.

Oil poured into those great cups holding the Earth's waters behaves in much the same way as in your cup. First, the oil from a spill rises to the surface. Then *weathering* — the action of the wind, waves, tides, currents, rains — stirs up the oil-water mixture. The oil mixes with the water, becomes heavier, and finally sinks to the bottom, where eventually it is decomposed by bacterial action — a step further than what you see in your cup.

Oil remaining on top of the water is acted upon by bacteria and also by sunlight, which burns off or *oxidizes* some of the chemicals in the oil. Spray or bursting bubbles and atmospheric pressure release more hydrocarbons into the air in the process of *evaporation*. Half to three-quarters of a spill on open water is dispersed by these natural processes. The oil that is left may wind up as a form of mousse, usually a mix of one-third oil and two-thirds water, or as a more weathered, tarry substance, moving with the tides and currents, perhaps to be caught on rocks or plants or washed up on beaches.

Exactly what happens in a spill depends on a multitude of variables. There are different oils, different environments, different climates. The petroleum product spilled can be light, such as gasoline, naphtha, benzene. Or it can be a heavy crude oil or fuel oil. Fuel oils can vary in heaviness — #2 oil is lighter than residential fuel oil, #6 is the heaviest, a sludgelike bunker oil used

Closeup of tar balls.

Oiled beach—this in Chile.

to fuel the engines of ships. Still other variables are the age of the spill and how much it has weathered, the temperature and movement of the air and of the water, and the kind of water — open or sheltered, salt or fresh, bottomed by sand or mud or rocks. The land can be swamp, marsh, rockbound coast, sandy beach; it can be deserted or a resort area. The season of the year, the weather, the state of the animal and plant life — all are variables to contend with in a spill.

Because of all the variables, the size of an oil spill may be disproportionate to its damage. The oil from the biggest spill the world has yet seen, from Ixtoc I, did less damage to the Texas shore than a very much smaller spill from the tanker *Burmah Agate*. The *Burmah Agate* collided with a freighter, the *Mimosa*, off Galveston in

Oiled vegetation in a marsh. This is heavy oil—it stays above ground.

the fall of 1979, killing 32 men. High winds stopped all attempts at water cleanup. Before shore operations could have any impact, much of the oil sank into the beach sand, to seep for years. The oil was less weathered and therefore more liquid and lighter than Ixtoc I oil, and lighter petroleum products sink deeper into porous ground than do heavy oils.

Spills of lighter oil, therefore, do more damage to roots of plants and to burrowing animals, and can also seep deep enough to reach groundwater. And *groundwater*, the water beneath the Earth's surface that supplies wells and springs, becomes drinking water. Whether petroleum hydrocarbons in drinking water are dangerous to human beings is not completely known. However, scientists have found *PNAs*, polynuclear aro-

matic hydrocarbons, in drinking water. PNAs are probably *carcinogens* or cancer-causing substances, and PNAs
are found in small amounts in crude oil and particularly
in benzene. And benzene is a light petroleum product.

Heavy oils like crude oil tend to stay on top of the
ground, and although there is some seepage, generally
it does not go deep. Vegetation and insects can be suf-
focated by the heavy oil, however. And animals who
feed on plants may be deprived of their food supply and
starve. Or they may feed on oiled vegetation and be
poisoned. The coats of animals are matted as they move
through the heavy oil, making it difficult for them to find
food or escape enemies. Also, when fur or feathers are
matted, the skin below is unprotected, and the animal
can die of exposure. Oil may also prevent eggs from
hatching or cause deformities in the newborn. There is
little danger, however, that an entire species will be
threatened by oil, except in the case of an already endangered species such as the jackass penguin of South
Africa or the whooping crane. The whooping crane unfortunately chooses to live near the spill-prone waters of
the Texas Gulf coast but fortunately, by some natural
instinct, goes inland to lay its eggs.

Instinct does not protect diving and swimming
sea birds from entering oiled waters. To the contrary,
the oil makes the water invitingly tranquil, and when
the birds dive they are burned or poisoned by the oil.
The fish and other animals of the sea can usually swim
away the second they sense a slick, but the birds cannot.
Neither can the slow-moving mollusks — clams, oysters,
and mussels. Crustaceans like the shrimp can even live
happily in areas of chronic oil spills, in the Gulf of Mex-

Heavy (#6) industrial heating oil spilled into the icy Hudson River in New York and proved extremely difficult to clean up. The oil froze or was embedded in ice.

ico. But an acute spill, a sudden large influx of oil from a blowout, will kill the crustaceans in the immediate area. However, it may not be the oil that does the killing as much as the brine that escapes with the oil in a blowout.

The effects of a spill on life are not always so visible or knowable. Oiled birds may not be able to complete migratory flights and go down unseen, many miles from a spill. Animals may not be able to communicate with one another to mate, or, like the salmon, the striped bass, the shad, may not be able to get to the waters they must reach to spawn. Plants and animals that cooperate with one another to provide food, protection, reproductive materials, may lose the services of their partners in nature, and die. An example is the guillemot, a sea bird whose excretions, rich in potash, fertilize plant life at the bottom of the sea and provide nutrients for microorganisms there. In the *Torrey Canyon* spill, tens of thousands of guillemots were killed. What then happened to the vegetation and microorganisms at the bottom of the sea, and to the species dependent on them? Change in the population in the sea may have consequences on life reaching far beyond the time and place of a spill, but we may never know them.

When, in April 1977, an offshore well blew out in the North Sea, it was feared that the oil would do great damage to the plankton in the area. *Zooplankton,* tiny, often microscopic, floating animals, spawn in the North Sea in the spring. They and their plant counterparts, *phytoplankton,* are the main source of food for many sea animals, including the mighty whale. If the plankton were destroyed, the results would spread throughout the life in the sea. Fortunately, the April of the blowout was unusually cold, and the zooplankton were slow in reaching the sea. By the time they arrived, the well had been capped. So the zooplankton spawned and served their purpose in life: to be eaten by other animals, which in turn are eaten by others, in a great food chain or web of eater-eaten, predator-prey relationships that reaches up to humankind. But what if the weather had been normal and the zooplankton caught by the oil?

If plants or animals in a food chain are killed in unusual numbers, the link they make is destroyed. Those below the broken link in the chain will flourish — they will not be eaten. Those above the broken link will have to find something else to eat, or they will die. If the zooplankton had been killed by the North Sea spill, there would have been a great increase in the bacteria and other nutrients they feed on. The whales and other sea life that feed on zooplankton would have had to find other food by moving out of the North Sea area or die of starvation. Thus the population in the sea changes as one species flourishes, another is depleted. This changing pattern of life has gone on since the world began — on land as well as in the sea, before oil spills, before human beings.

Human beings are also part of the food chain, and petroleum hydrocarbons run up and down that chain. We do not know how many petroleum hydrocarbons we ingest, but if we were to encounter a fish on our dinner plates that had an unusually large amount of petroleum hydrocarbons in it, the smell and taste would turn us off — we'd refuse to eat it. However, water and certain foods like lettuce and mushrooms sometimes contain even more hydrocarbons of petroleum from petroleum-based fertilizers and rain fallout than the fish we refuse. We can't taste these hydrocarbons, however — their flavor and smell have been left behind in the earth — and so we digest them, seemingly with little or no adverse result. There are those who disagree, but the fact of the matter is that we have no proofs one way or the other.

The research goes on, however, and perhaps one day we will know the answers to our questions about petroleum and life.

CHAPTER

5

The Watchdogs

In January 1969, in the Santa Barbara channel off the California coast, an underwater blowout of an oil well caused heavy damage. Above-water blowouts are usually stopped by the fire that accompanies them, but an underwater blowout like that at Santa Barbara is hard to stop.

Almost two years had passed since the country's concern was aroused by the *Torrey Canyon* disaster — concern quickly forgotten as someone else's problem. But this time the damage hit home. This time it was in *our* waters, and a particularly beautiful shoreline was damaged in a particularly wealthy section of the country. Action was demanded, and promptly obtained from Washington.

The National Environmental Policy Act (NEPA) of 1969 established a national policy for the environment and provided for the establishment of a Council on Environmental Quality responsible directly to the President. NEPA concerns itself with the means to improve the conditions in which human beings can exist in harmony with nature. A very broad and vague directive, it gains impact by providing for all federal agencies to consider the environmental impact of *all* proposed actions. NEPA also requires the filing of Environmental Impact Statements as a controlling and measuring process, and in 1970, an Executive Order was issued that all executive agencies cooperate in furthering the provisions of NEPA.

Also in 1970, the Federal Water Pollution Control Act prohibited the deliberate discharge of oil or hazardous substances into or upon the navigable waters of the United States, its adjoining shorelines, or the waters of the contiguous zone. The contiguous zone reaches out 200 miles from our national boundaries.

An amendment to this Act in 1972 and an Executive Order in 1973 assigned prevention, detection, and cleaning of oil spills and spills of other hazardous substances to the United States Coast Guard, an agency of the Department of Transportation, and the newly created Environmental Protection Agency (EPA). The Coast Guard has authority over transportation-related facilities, including those on land; the EPA's authority is over stationary facilities such as oil fields and tank farms and offshore oil wells.

The Oil Pollution Act and its Amendments cover restrictions on discharge of oil and oily wastes in specified sea areas worldwide. The Act specifically exempts vessels of the United States Navy from compliance because of the military nature of their mission, but the Navy does adhere to the Act's requirements when feasible. The Navy's own stated policy is to eliminate all spills from its ships and other facilities, and they have a multitude of rules and regulations to that end. The Navy develops and tests its own preventive and cleanup equipment, cleans its own spills, and pursues its own environmental protection program — all, of course, within federal directives and laws. It also cooperates with other agencies when needed in a spill cleanup, to provide aerial surveillance or manpower.

Massive spills require such a great amount of manpower and equipment that the use of troops and military logistics is usually necessary. The Department of Defense is therefore considered a "primary agency" in spill response. The Defense Department is also responsible for the maintenance of navigation channels, salvage, and removal of navigational obstructions.

Other primary agencies are the Department of Transportation and the Department of Commerce, which has NOAA within its jurisdiction. NOAA, National Oceanic and Atmospheric Administration, does research on the environmental impact of spills and provides information to cleanup teams on ocean, coastal, and inland waters, and details on the marine environment and its living resources. The Department of the Interior is still another primary agency. It administers the United States Geological Survey, the agency whose expertise is in oil drilling and producing and in pipeline administration. The National Wildlife Service, responsible for supervision of bird cleanup operations, is also part of the Department of the Interior.

Backup roles are played by other governmental agencies. The Department of Justice supplies legal advice on the many questions of conflicting laws and compensation for damages and other points of law. The Department of State develops international agreements and provides coordination in spills involving international boundaries and foreign ships. HUD, the Department of Housing and Urban Development, has local environmental branches and a Federal Disaster Assistance Administration to coordinate and direct federal response in major disasters.

Then there are agencies whose work is more or less peripheral to the problem of spills. The National Air Pollution Control Administration, for instance, focuses not on oil in the sea but on vehicle emissions in the air. However, as we have seen, those gases from burning gasoline and diesel and jet fuels fall into the sea as hydrocarbons of petroleum. So, whoever or whatever controls engine emissions controls ten percent of the oil that reaches the sea every year.

We have an impressive array of concerned federal agencies, regulations, rules, directives, acts, memorandums of procedure, and executive orders. Most state and city and some local governments have also set up their own agencies and departments and formulated their own regulations for the prevention and cleanup of spills. Virtually all states include specifics of financial responsibility and compensation. New York State, for instance, has a law on oil-spill prevention, control, and compensation that deals almost exclusively with money. License fees of 1¢ a barrel of petroleum established a fund of $25 million for spill compensation, and operators of major facilities are required to post proof of financial responsibility of several million dollars to insure that the costs of cleanup will be paid by them.

Then there are private regulations controlling industry practices. The petroleum and shipping industries have programs of prevention and maintain cooperative strike teams for cleanup. The American Petroleum Institute, the Oil Pollution Control Association of America, shipowners, railways — all are committed to spill prevention and cleanup through policies raising standards of performance and doing research and disseminating information. Nobody — *nobody* — wants an oil spill. except Sadam

On the high seas, outside of any one country's jurisdiction, oil spills are an international problem and must be dealt with on that level. To give you an idea of how complicated this can be, consider once again the *Torrey Canyon*. You've already read about many of the problems faced and decisions made by several countries on how to clean up the oil. Even before cleanup began there were many other problems and vital decisions to be made.

When the *Torrey Canyon* went aground, that ground, the Seven Stones, was British territory. But the Seven Stones is not in British waters, it's in international waters. If the *Torrey Canyon* was in international waters, was Britain responsible for the cleanup and damage claims? Was the tanker's owner? The ship was owned by a Bermudian tanker company. But she had been rented for the voyage by an American oil company. To complicate this relationship further, the American oil company owned the Bermudian tanker company! However, the *Torrey Canyon* was registered in Liberia. And her crew were all Italian, hired in Italy for the voyage.

Britain was not at all sure that cleanup was her job. But as the oil threatened her shores, she had to move, whatever the legalities of the situation, and so did each of the afflicted countries in turn. Compensation could be taken care of later. Ultimately, investigations and claims hearings were held in — can you guess? — Liberia, the country of registration, and Italy, the crew's home. The situation was not made easier by the distances and the different laws of each country involved.

As a result of the *Torrey Canyon* confusion, four basic international agreements were reached. Essentially, the agreements stipulate that the country where the oil touches down will clean it up; the spiller will pay costs and damages. This doesn't mean the spiller *accepts* responsibility. Mexico, for instance, refused to pay cleanup costs incurred by the United States for cleaning up the Texas shoreline of the Ixtoc I oil. The United States, they said, had contaminated the New River that runs from Baja California into the United States with garbage and didn't clean up. Nor did the United States compensate Mexico for the saline water from the Colorado River that caused salt beds to form in the Mexicali Valley, ruining farmland.

The United Nations has two groups concerned with oil pollution in international waters. One hundred and three member nations belong to IMCO, the Intergovernmental Maritime Consultative Organization. IMCO was already in existence at the time of the *Torrey Canyon* spill, and Great Britain called on it to outline better traffic rules for ships in international waters. Functioning within IMCO is the Marine Environment Protection Committee, which has set up standards for disposing of vessel sewage, garbage, and oil cargo wastes. The Committee also gathers scientific, technical, and practicable information on the marine environment.

GESAMP, the Joint Group of Experts on the Scientific Aspects of Marine Pollution, is the other agency of the United Nations working on marine pollution. GESAMP and IMCO provide a forum for airing problems, and have set up international conventions for regulating maritime safety and efficiency.

Outside the United Nations, the 1954 Convention for the Prevention of Pollution of the Sea by Oil is the only international convention that has been ratified. It prohibits dumping of oil in international waters. A 1973 convention, still not ratified and therefore without the force of law, provides for the elimination of all forms of international dumping. It also calls for ship construction permitting separate oil and water storage, to eliminate the spilling of oily ballast water. It also provides that ports have reception facilities for oily wastes.

The length of time it takes to ratify a convention, to satisfy the demands of 103 countries, makes international law extremely difficult. Even when ratified, conventions lack the power of enforcement. This would require an international marine police force, and no one seems ready for that yet. So obedience to a convention is really voluntary.

Other international agreements of a limited nature exist. The Trans-Alaska Pipeline Fund, a compensation fund, provides for payment for environmental damage by any ship carrying pipeline oil along the coast of the United States and Canada. The United States and Canada have an agreement that provides for joint cleanup of spills on waterways between the two countries. In June 1976, 300,000 gallons of oil spilled in the St. Lawrence River. In accordance with the agreement, Canada and the United States each cleaned its own side.

Tanker trails oil on the St. Lawrence River after collision.

Oil (light patches) threatens heavily populated islands in the St. Lawrence River spill. Barrier between two points of land *(center)* keeps most of oil away from inlet.

High-school students volunteered to help clean St. Lawrence spill. Here they are cutting and hauling away oiled grasses. Today, cutting is used primarily for cosmetic reasons rather than for cleanup. Grasses can act as sponges and prevent further damage, so cutting serves no real purpose. Damage can also be increased by the incursion of humans and equipment.

And then, beyond the terms of the agreement, Canada trucked over the border to help its neighbor in the manner of friends. Friends they had to be, because cleanup was largely done by hand with rags and putty knives.

The United States also has an agreement with the Soviet Union for joint laboratory testing and field studies by the EPA and the Ministry of the Merchant Marine at Leningrad.

And watching over all the laws, all the efforts,

watching over the watchdog agencies, watching governments nationally and internationally, watching industry, there are the conservationists and environmentalists and concerned citizens. Some are organized into groups such as the Audubon and Sierra Societies, many are unorganized, but they are all vitally interested. And concerned citizenry has political pressure that can move mountains — or oil from our troubled waters.

CHAPTER

6

An Ounce
of Prevention . . .

Most oil spills can be prevented — at least, that's what
the United States government says. So a large part of the
fight against pollution by oil is waged out of the public
view, in the prosaic arenas of prevention: education,
lawmaking, standard-setting, and safeguarding.

Programs of prevention concern themselves primarily with human error. Government sources report
that 85 percent of all spills can be traced to human error:
somebody, somewhere, did something wrong. Someone
got drunk, didn't understand a command or a procedure,
made the wrong decision. One hundred thirty-five thousand gallons of oil spilled into the Chesapeake Bay
when a workman in charge of oil-loading operations fell
asleep. Someone misjudged the amount of pressure
needed to compensate for withdrawing a worn drill bit
and caused the Santa Barbara spill. Someone neglected
to supply Ixtoc I with heavy drilling mud. This mud is
needed to stop the sudden gushing forth of oil when a
drill bit breaks open the rocks that have held the liquid

in check for millions of years. Someone on the *Torrey Canyon* neglected to train the crewman in proper handling of the wheel, and the captain himself plotted the ship's course incorrectly. . . .

Human beings provide themselves with machines and other devices to help them cope with potentially difficult problems, and handlers of oil are no exception. But behind all the mechanical techniques — the radar, the alarm systems, the automatic shutdown valves, the blowout preventers, the thousands of other aids — are human beings who control them. Special X-ray cameras and electronic instruments of high complexity show the insides of a pipeline, but people have to recognize whether that shadow they see is a crack or patch of erosion or just a shadow.

Train the people who use the machines, the devices, the instruments, educate those who handle the oil, build safeguards against human error, and — abracadabra! — that gigantic 85 percent figure will be eliminated. The mud will always be there when needed, the pressure will be properly compensated for, the crewman will handle himself properly, no one will get drunk or fall asleep on the job. That would be very nice, if it were possible. Of course, no one seriously believes that human error can be completely eliminated, but they're sure it can be reduced.

To that end, industry, government agencies, and schools like Texas A&M and Texas A&I offer on-the-job training, classroom instruction, practice drills, and other programs aimed at reducing human error by increasing awareness and skills. The American Petroleum Institute and the University of Texas co-sponsor classes in oil-

spill prevention, including the use of complex electronic instruments safeguarding pipelines. Ships' mas-
ters and pilots learn the intricacies of new equipment
and ports from simulators or mockups and film pro-
jections to prevent accidents that might cause spills.
Oil-well operators put their people through periodic
blowout prevention drills. There are training courses for
drivers of tank trucks on how to fill service-station and
home fuel tanks. (Unfortunately there is no anti-spill
education for homeowners or other members of the general public, although a few states have set up oily waste
collection units to encourage proper disposal.)

Coast Guard representatives sit in conference
with ships' crews before major oil transfer operations to
make sure that every step is clearly understood ahead of
time by everyone involved. Operating procedures are
also posted in the various languages understood by the
crews.

Facilities and vessels concerned with oil cannot
function, nor can an exploratory well be drilled, without
an elaborately outlined plan for safety and personnel
training known as a Spill Prevention Control and Coun-
termeasure (SPCC) Plan. The government requires that
an SPCC Plan be prepared by all facilities that have
discharged — or could reasonably be expected to discharge — oil in harmful quantities.

The prevention battle is not directed at human
error alone. All kinds of devices are in operation and are
constantly being developed to prevent spills and leaks.
Culverts and gutters drain off oil to diversion and retention ponds for collection; and walls, dikes, and berms
(narrow ledges) are placed strategically for retention of

oil on land installations. Booms or floating barriers, are put down permanently at spill-prone facilities to keep oil from spreading in the water. Oil-water separators are used at oil rigs and refineries and at the newer storage terminals, so that even the smallest of spills can be recovered. And those small spills can add up.

More ships are allowing oil to separate out of the water used to clean tanks or as ballast before flushing it into the sea. This spares the environment and saves thousands of dollars' worth of oil per voyage. The system has its drawbacks: it can be used only on voyages long enough and smooth enough for the oil to separate out; and, no matter how carefully done, it is difficult to determine the point at which only water is being pumped out, so that some oil is inevitably spilled. Some ships are using crude oil under pressure instead of water to hose off sludge in the tanks. All the oil remains in the tanker, nothing at all has to be dumped into the water, and the crude oil seems to clean better than water.

Newly constructed United States tankers must have separate ballast tanks so ballast water is never mixed with oil on the sides of cargo tanks. New tankers must also have double hulls to prevent puncturing of cargo tanks if the ship is grounded or in a collision. Of course, even a double hull can be pierced, so there is some debate over the value of this requirement as a preventive measure. At present, it is an academic question — few new tankers are being built, except for special ice-breaking tankers for the new drilling areas in the far North. Hundreds of supertankers sit in ship graveyards, never used, built in a monumental miscalculation of numbers needed. To refit tankers already built would be far too expensive. More important, extensive rebuilding might endanger the structure of the ship.

Vessel safety is of vital importance in preventing spills. Design, construction, and maintenance standards for United States tankers and other merchant ships are high and are strictly monitored by the Coast Guard.

Since 1972, the Coast Guard also requires certain construction standards and operating procedures for all foreign ships entering United States territorial waters. Coast Guard representatives board every ship, sometimes at sea, more often in port, to inspect for compliance and can detain violaters — an expensive proposition for shipowners, who can lose as much as $10,000 a day when a ship is laid up. Most tankers and other merchant ships fly *flags of convenience* — are registered in countries like Panama or Liberia. Owners of these ships save on registration fees, shipyard costs, non-union crews, and insurance premiums. Nor do they need to meet expensive construction criteria and safety standards, and many of these flag-of-convenience ships are overworked, aged, neglected tubs, barely seaworthy.

On December 15, 1976, such a tanker, the S.S. *Argo Merchant*, flying the Liberian flag, ran aground 35 miles southeast of Nantucket Island, Massachusetts. Just short of her destination port, she was off course and in dangerous waters. According to her captain, the few navigation aids she carried did not function properly. It was the last episode in a long history of mishaps and infractions in the *Argo Merchant*'s years at sea. The *Argo Merchant* finally broke up on December 21, spilling over 7,700,000 gallons of heavy industrial oil, the largest spill ever to threaten United States shores. Cleanup was im-

A Coast Guard cutter, the *Vigilant*, arrives to assist the grounded *Argo Merchant*. Crew members were evacuated over a two-day period.

A Coast Guard helicopter hovers over the *Argo Merchant.*

possible because of high winds and building waves. Fortunately, those winds and waves and currents moved most of the oil out to sea rather than onto the beaches. However, some of the oil moved into one of the world's great fishing areas, Georges Bank, threatening a large fishing industry and the humpback whales and gray seals in the area — a threat that was largely and happily unrealized.

As a result of the *Argo Merchant* spill, the Coast

Six days after grounding, building seas whipped by high winter winds break the *Argo Merchant* apart.

Guard can refuse entry to U.S. ports of foreign-flag vessels that fail detailed checks of structure and of fire-fighting and cargo-handling equipment. Foreign ships must also have on board the most essential of navigational aids: a magnetic compass, a gyrocompass, a depth finder, a radio direction finder, and radar — all in good working condition. It is hard to believe that ships crossing oceans today would not have such basic instruments without the Coast Guard demanding them.

The federal judge who was to rule on damages after a three-year trial said, "The possibility suggests itself that the shipowner, through the agency of the captain and perhaps the other officers, intentionally grounded the vessel. . . ." Such possibilities are not unknown when worn-out ships are worth more for their insurance than for their labor.

Upgrading conditions on these old tankers is important, but scrapping them would be better. Why not eliminate the need for lightering by building ports to accommodate supertankers? LOOP (Louisiana Off-shore Oil Port) and superports off the Texas and Virginia coasts are in various stages of completion — and financial problems: superports are super-expensive. There are other areas in the United States with the capacity for superports, but there is little movement toward developing them. Aside from the financial complexities, there is also the public's fear of supertankers and their spill potential. Of course, a supertanker can cause one super spill, but statistics show that more oil is spilled from small tankers. Experts view supertankers, with their highly advanced engineering and safety standards and their trained crews, as far safer than conventional tankers, but it is hard to convince the public of this. For instance, Puget Sound, Washington, bans ships of more than 125,000 tons. (Whether this is legal — whether a state can make restrictive laws for waterways in interstate commerce — is a question being decided in the Supreme Court.) At the same time, however, Puget Sound is equipped with a system for port safety, Vessel Traffic Service or VTS, that a fearful public in some other areas is trying to ban, citing the possible danger from microwave emissions. VTS is a radar tracking system for harbor traffic, and its purpose is to prevent collisions in busy harbors. Each vessel arriving at a VTS harbor reports in to a traffic control center on shore. The control center assigns the ship a course through the port to her docking space and informs her of traffic along the way. Checkpoints keep ship and shore in contact and everything in its proper place.

VTS has been used in most European ports for years, but in the United States its use is limited. Since each port must approve its installation, the VTS has become something of an environmental and political football. VTS is installed in the ports of San Francisco, Houston, New Orleans, Valdez, and a partial system is operating in New York City. New York VTS was delayed for years. At first, it was a matter of appearance — a radar tower was to be erected in an affluent residential area. Then the tower became an environmentalist issue because of microwave emissions. Despite proofs from its manufacturer, and Coast Guard reassurances that the tower emitted far fewer microwaves than the telephone and telegraph installations that concern no one, the issue became much publicized and local politicians played with it happily. The lifesaving aspect of VTS, its importance in preventing shipping accidents and oil spills (which also radiate microwaves), was overlooked in the circus atmosphere the issue presented. We do not know if microwaves in the atmosphere — or petroleum hydrocarbons in water — present a long-term threat to life. Unfortunately, too many environmental issues such as this are obscured in rhetoric propounded by cause-hungry groups with limited perspectives. Vested interest and self-serving causes, whatever their source, can seriously limit real investigation. Is microwave emission more serious than ship collisions? Are its proponents truthful or self-serving for profit? Will the same groups who fight against superports or VTS join the general

VTS is expected to eliminate harbor collisions like this one between a tanker and freighter in fog. Sixteen persons were killed here.

clamor when there is a ship collision or breakdown that causes oil to pollute the oceans?

Not that VTS or superports mean absolute security against spills. They can only limit, not resolve, problems. No matter what the United States government says, oil spills are not completely preventable. Earthquakes and eruptive volcanoes like Mount St. Helens may rupture pipelines and petroleum storage tanks. Cruise ships like the luxury liner *Prinsendam* somehow catch on fire and sink, carrying 200,000 gallons of fuel to the bottom of the Gulf of Alaska. Insurance fraud will entice the unscrupulous to ground ships. And human error will always be with us, perhaps lessened but never eradicated. So will other human frailties, and so will the vagaries of wind and weather. Until the world runs out of oil, or develops alternatives to oil, there will be oil spills.

7

A Deciliter
of Detection

The everyday work of the EPA and Coast Guard in preventing spills, the inspecting and challenging and checking, get very little attention from anyone but abusive spillers, angry citizens, and wild dogs in the wastelands bordering sewer outlets and deserted piers. The work is difficult, tedious, and sometimes downright dangerous. Coast Guard inspectors have been known to fall into the water while collecting samples to detect oil. They have plunged through rotting docks and been made sick from gases in the sewers they have to check for draining oil. They've gasped their way up 50-foot ladders to board rocking tankers, then choked for air as they descended into the bowels of a ship, risking deafness in the thundering din of the pump room. They have braved ice and gale winds and boiling heat, covering the waterfront by tugboat or on foot, scrambling onto barges and boats, poking into drainage ditches, checking hoses and piping and machinery and gauges and safety devices — all to keep oil from reaching water.

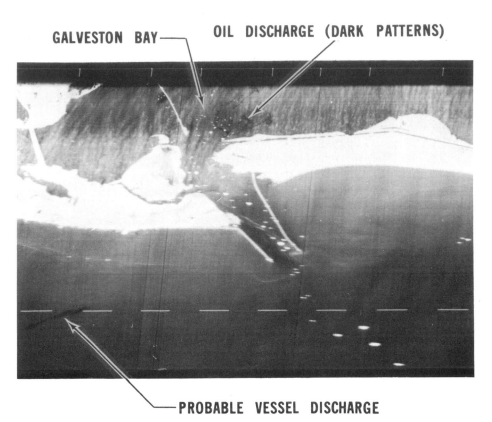

GALVESTON BAY—— OIL DISCHARGE (DARK PATTERNS)

——PROBABLE VESSEL DISCHARGE

An AOSS radar view of the entrance to Galveston (Texas) harbor.

Inspectors can't be everywhere, so aerial surveillance and monitoring systems are used to detect spills. The Coast Guard Airborne Oil Surveillance System, AOSS, provides for systematic inspection by air for signs of oil on the water. A plane can "read" a spill at distances of up to 25 miles on each side of it by four basic methods: side-viewing radar, which distinguishes the smooth slick from the rougher water around it; an infrared scanner that detects differences in the temperatures of oil and water; an ultraviolet scanner to pick up ultraviolet rays the oil reflects; and an instrument that records patterns of microwaves emitted by oil.

66

Oil sensors are used where constant surveillance is needed. The sensors are installed in harbors and inland waterways, near refineries and industrial complexes, and at sites where oil-transfer operations and bilge-emptying take place. The sensors use infrared, fluorescent ultraviolet, and reflected ultraviolet rays as well as laser light to detect the luminosity, or sheen, of oil in the water. Sensors also pick up indications of oil in vapors from the differences in evaporation times of oil and water.

Continuous monitoring is so important for early detection and thus more successful cleanup, that satellite monitoring from space is being attempted by the Coastal Zone Color Scanner.

On a more down-to-earth level, every ship and plane is asked to watch for signs of oil spills. You, too, are encouraged to report spills by calling your local EPA office or Coast Guard installation, or by calling the national oil spill hotline, 1-800-424-0201, toll-free, of course.

Spillers are expected to report their spills. Many, however, do not want to bear the cost of cleanup or fines, so they avoid reporting, hoping to escape detection. On the other hand, some spillers report so quickly that the spills turn out to be false alarms! These spillers operate on the theory that "it's better to be safe than sorry." That's because the Water Pollution Control Act is somewhat easier on the self-confessed spiller. The Act calls for fines of up to $5000 if a ship or other facility causes a spill and reports it; if unreported, the fine is $10,000 — *if* the spiller gets caught and is judged responsible.

One Oklahoma oil well operator who did the

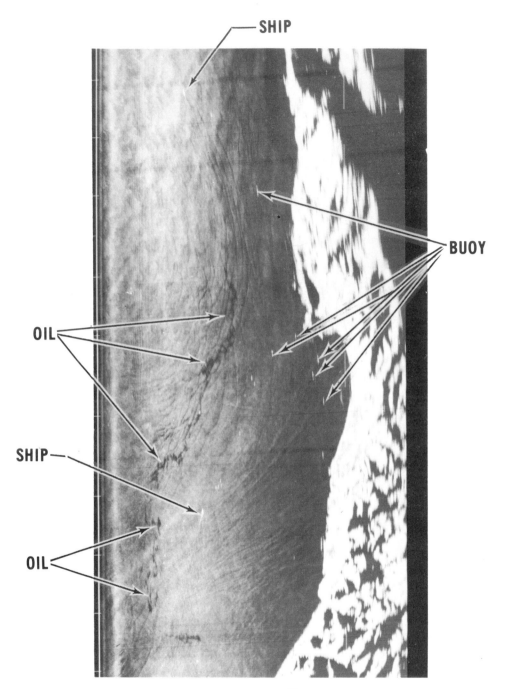

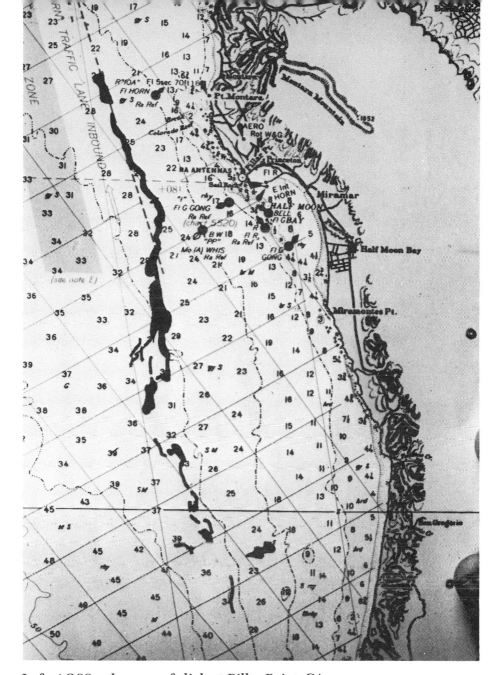

Left: AOSS radar map of slick at Pillar Point, CA.
Right: Same slick, showing exact distribution of oil on a grid chart.

proper thing, reported a spill for which he was responsible, was fined $500 for his trouble. He fought the fine and the Water Pollution Control Act all the way to the Supreme Court. He argued that reporting the spill was, in effect, being forced to incriminate himself, a violation of his constitutional rights. The Supreme Court didn't agree with him. The Court ruled that the principle of self-incrimination applied only to criminal charges, and oil-spill responsibility was a civil matter rather than a criminal one. The Water Pollution Control Act provisions were therefore constitutional.

Many spills are unreported "mystery spills." Often these spills come from ships cleaning bilges and cargo tanks in defiance of the law. One famous mystery spill, in July of 1975, washed up 50,000 gallons of oil onto the island-dotted shoreline of the Florida Keys. The Coast Guard went on a monumental search for the culprit, checking hundreds of ships and ports from Maine to Texas, taking samples of oil from the holds of suspect ships. The samples were then matched against a specimen of the spilled oil. This can be done because the variations in chemical composition and the effects of storage make every oil distinctive. The oil is identified by a four-part method involving infrared and ultraviolet light, iodine vapors, super-high pressure, and temperatures as low as $-321°$ F. to as hot as flaming hydrogen. The structure of the oil can be plotted as a line on a graph. Like fingerprints, no two graphs are exactly alike unless they are of the same oil from the same ship or storage tank.

Six months of fingerprinting over 200 oils, and other detective work, finally paid off when the Coast

Preparing oil samples for analysis.

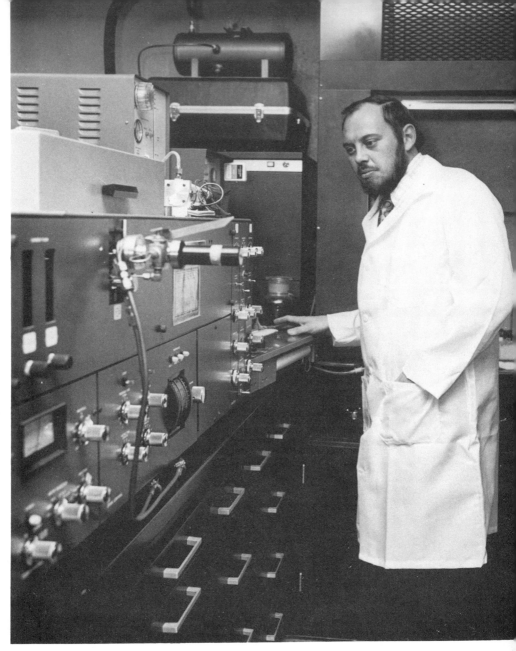

Using computerized gas chromatographic analysis for oil identification. The oil is distilled and the molecules emerge at different times, allowing for identification of their structure.

Chromatographic developing chamber, ultraviolet light box, and plate storage container used for identification of oil spills by thin layer chromatography. Under ultraviolet light the different fluorescent colored bands of the compounds of particular oils become visible.

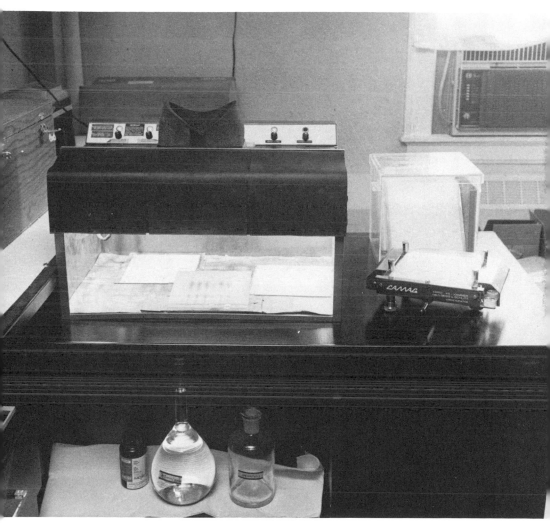

Guard identified the Florida Keys oil as coming from the Liberian-registered tanker *Garbis*. The captain admitted his guilt and was arrested. Criminal charges were dropped, however, when the captain contended that the oil had been spilled in international waters, where the

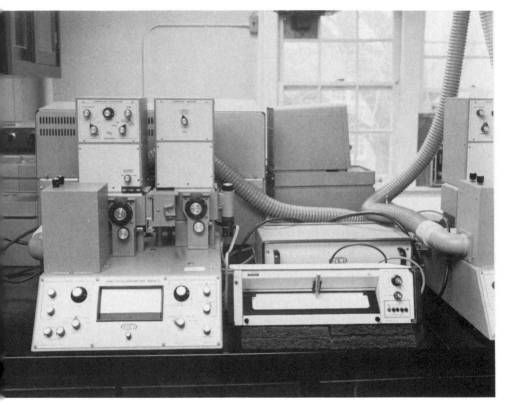

The spectrofluorometer, graphing device on right. Fluorescent spectroscopy involves exposure of oil sample to ultraviolet light. The oil absorbs the light and then emits it, giving an easily read profile of the fluorescent compounds of oil. Infrared spectroscopy involves passing infrared beams through an oil smear between two sheets of solid salt. The beam is then measured for the amount of energy absorbed.

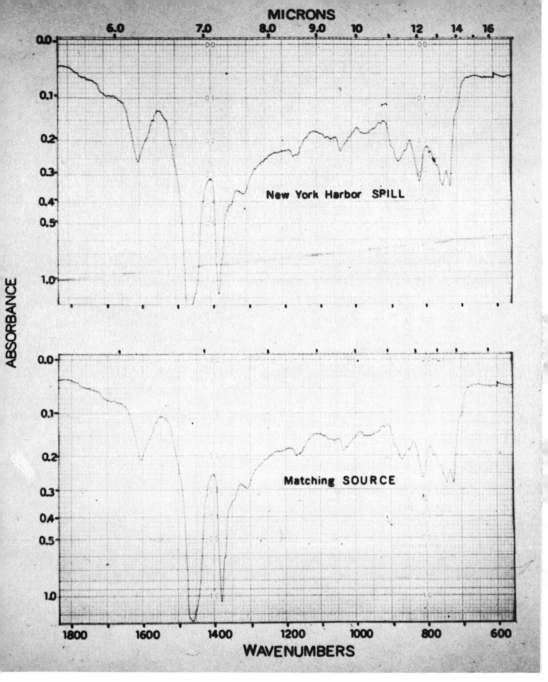

Fingerprinted!

law prohibiting deliberate spills did not apply, and had drifted into Florida waters. No one could prove differently. The Coast Guard effort was not completely in vain despite this setback. It did serve notice that an authority was watching — often an effective deterrent.

Not only machines are used to detect sources of oil — mussels do it, too! Mussels extract pollutants as well as nutrients from the water passing over their gills. Something about mussel physiology concentrates pollutants up to one million times, so, in controlled groups, the mussels can collect specific pollutants like oil and can even give clues to sources. The United States has some 105 collection sites for monitoring oil and other pollution with mussel sensors, and researchers hope to extend these sites worldwide.

8

. . . A Pound of Cure

Every spill is different from every other spill. The kind and amount of petroleum spilled will vary widely: there are tens of thousands of crude, refined, and residual oils. The spill area will be almost as variable. There are wetlands — swamp, marsh — and rocky, sandy, plant-covered lands. The area can be sheltered or open, farmland or marina, populated or unpopulated. Water can be salt, fresh, or briny (a combination), open or enclosed, cold or warm, still or rough, close to shore or breeding grounds. There may be ice — and oil can be frozen into it, running under it, sandwiched between layers, or mixed with snow. Winds may be high, low, or gale-force; currents may be fast or of different temperatures. Cleanup choices must be based on all these factors and more.

Manpower and equipment available to do the job must be taken into consideration, as well as who pays for the cleanup. While the spiller is technically responsible for payment, there may be factors, such as lack of money or the extent of the spill, making it impossible.

To bring some kind of order to this multitude of

possibilities in a spill cleanup, *contingency plans* are formulated in many high-risk areas. A contingency plan outlines the geography and key points of the area and the kinds of wildlife and vegetation, with their particular sensitivities. The plan lays down precise responsibilities and duties in the event of a spill, and the equipment on hand or available locally. In other words, a battle plan is drawn up to save time, prevent confusion, and help win the day against an invasion of oil.

The United States has an international contingency plan with Canada, discussed on page 49. A National Oil and Hazardous Substances Contingency Plan for the United States was prepared by the Council on Environmental Quality, which is also responsible for its updating. Under this Plan, the EPA and the Coast Guard are given the authority for developing and putting into practice local and regional contingency plans. Every federal department and agency concerned with oil is also authorized to form its own contingency plan. All plans, including those drawn up by private companies, are supposed to coordinate with the National Contingency Plan. That they do not is a source of confusion and a problem slowly being remedied.

A National Spill Response Team serves as an overall body for planning and preparedness. The Team also provides coordination and advice in a major spill emergency. Based in a National Response Center in Washington, D.C., the Team has Regional Response Centers placed strategically around the country to provide personnel and facilities and act as a command center for cleanup operations. Teams based at these centers are automatically called to duty in the event of a poten-

Regional Response Team in emergency session.

tial or actual major spill and determine the duration and extent of federal response. A designated On-Site Coordinator (OSC) is placed in charge at the actual site of the spill — the battlefield commander supervising the fight and in turn reporting to the high command at the Response Center.

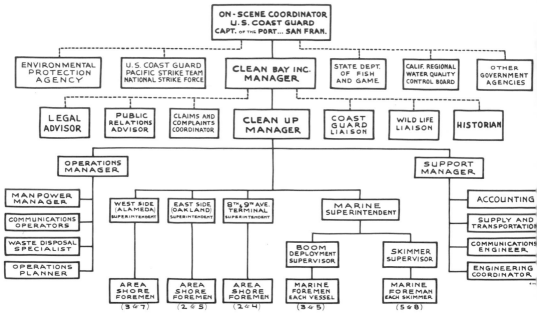

* ORGANIZATION VARIED FROM DAY TO DAY and DAY TO NIGHT...DEPENDING ON LOGISTICS OF OPERATIONS

Organization chart for contingency planning.

By law the Coast Guard and EPA must respond to all reports of spills of a gallon or more. The extent of that response is determined by the On-Site Coordinator. Since the spiller is responsible for cleanup, the response of the spiller must be determined first. There are over 100 private cleanup strike forces sponsored on a cooperative basis by the various oil companies and headquartered strategically throughout the country. If the size of the spill and the hazards to the environment and to human safety dictate further response, the On-Site Coordinator will call up reinforcements, including the National Strike Force and the Environmental Response Team. At the Ixtoc I spill, a 75-member scientific unit of NOAA worked with a computer to advise on where to combat the oil, what animals to protect first, and to provide documentation for scientific organizations researching the spill.

The EPA's Environmental Response Team may include an ecologist, a marine biologist, a geologist, a soils engineer, a water chemist, and other specialists. The Coast Guard's National Strike Force is made up of three 20-man teams. A strike team will fly to spills wherever the National Response Center and On-Site Coordinator decide they are needed or where foreign governments request them. They are on 24-hour, 365-day alert, and can get to any spill in the United States within two hours. Foreign spills take a little longer — one must wait for an invitation! Beepers alert team members to emergencies. The men carry travelers checks, passports, and open orders wherever they go so they can be ready to take off for anywhere without frustrating delays. They pile on a C-130 cargo plane loaded with equipment, fly to the airfield nearest the spill, and then transfer to boats, helicopters, trucks, even parachutes — whatever means will get them to the spill site. Some of the men are divers, some machinery technicians, some experts in chemicals, some wildlife specialists. All are salvage and lifesaving experts. They work to control the flow of oil at its source, set up barriers to contain the spill, and take measures to clean it up.

The work of a strike force is dangerous. Harsh petroleum chemicals burn the skin, vapors anaesthetize and cause flash fires and explosions that maim and kill. Snakebite is not unknown. Days may be spent on a disabled ship without heat or light or sanitary facilities — as one strike team did for 43 days in the sub-Antarctic waters off Chile with freezing hurricane-force wind.

A strike team brings equipment to supplement that already on the site, hired locally from private contractors. Oil companies can supply cleanup equipment that they usually own cooperatively and they may or may not also rely on private contractors. Equipment falls into four major categories: containment, pickup, storage, and disposal.

CONTAINMENT

Containment of a spill on water is generally by *booms*, floating barriers. Oil will spread just so far, because it has a natural tendency to stay together rather than break up in blobs. Booms work best in quiet, protected waters — they are excellent for containing chronic spills in a harbor. If the oil is not too thin or the water is not moving too quickly, a stationary boom works well. If the water is moving quickly, the boom can be made to run with it but at just the right speed to keep the oil from escaping. Booms don't work in too high

82

The work of a strike team is not easy.

Boom being loaded onto a tug to be taken to spill site.

Moving booms. Light areas oil; dark, water.

water because the oil sweeps under. Booms aren't good in high waves either, because the oil sweeps over. Nor do booms work in "rainbow" spills — thin layers of oil that are little more than a sheen. You see rainbow spills in miniature in puddles on heavily trafficked streets after a rain.

The Coast Guard has a boom called the Open Water Oil Containment System. It shoots out onto the water like a jack-in-the-box and inflates automatically.

Open sea skimmer and containment boom at a platform fire in the Gulf of Mexico.

Low-pressure hosing in an attempt to clean ice and herd oil for pickup.

Other booms are connected in sections. Special bubblers can act as permanent booms in chronic spill areas. For booming in ice, the Navy recommends 4'x8' plywood sheets lodged in slots in the ice cut by hot-water jet hoses and then frozen in place.

Hosing oil from marshland.

Booms and low pressure hosing with water or air are also used as *herders* to move oil out of a current or to move scattered slicks together or off ice or grass for easier pickup. Chemical herders have also been developed. One, called "bregoil" and formulated by a Swed-

87

ish engineer, not only herds but absorbs oil as well. The U.S. Naval Research Laboratory uses a liquid herder called piston film that forms a very thin layer on top of the oil and stops it from spreading.

PICKUP OR REMOVAL

Once the oil has been contained, it can be picked up, sunk, burned, chemically dispersed, or even eaten. The choice of removal techniques depends on the nature of the spill and the threat it may present to the environment. Whenever possible, recovery of oil for future use is part of the removal or cleanup. Removal techniques all have good and bad points — there is simply no one good, effective, "magic" method of cleaning up oil.

Skimming the oil from the top of the water and removing it with vacuum or suction pumps is a favored cleanup method in the United States. Skimmers work best when the oil layer is thick, so they are usually used with boom herders. Skimming is not a new idea. As early as the 1920s, the United States outfitted a tanker with an experimental skimmer to retrieve oil from the water during deballasting operations. Today's skimmers may be fixed in place, as in an area where there is chronic spilling, or they may be moved like a vacuum cleaner or the continuous moving belt of tractor treads. Some skimmers are even self-propelled.

Most skimmers have oil-water separators in them so that the water they pick up can be released and the oil retained until it can be emptied into barges or porta-

Vacuum cleaner-type skimmer.

Skimmer in calm, shallow water.

The Cold Weather Oil Recovery System: a skimmer designed for use in ice, particularly in Alaska. The crane on the cutter in the background hoists the skimmer in and out of the water.

ble storage units on shore. There are skimmers with screens to keep out debris (but they also screen marine life out of the water) and debris grinders.

Skimmers come in small, medium, and large sizes. The choice of skimmers depends on the size of the spill, water conditions, the amount of debris in the

MARCO skimmer. Oil is picked up on a belt and transferred to storage tank inside skimmer. Coast Guard crew in background is using hose herding; Navy crewmen and private contractors man the skimmer.

water, how hard it is to get the skimmer to the spill — and on what skimmer happens to be on hand.

Skimmers are best used in large, open areas where vapors dissipate readily — the mechanics of a skimmer are such that they can cause a vapor explosion, and medium and large skimmers come equipped with

Explosimeters to warn of danger. There are other nega-tives. Skimmers do not work properly in winds of over two knots — little more than dead calm. And, at the present time, skimmers do not work in waves of over two feet. Instead of rising and falling with the wave, conforming to its pattern, skimmers go straight through, missing the oil that has risen to the top of the water.

Pumping is a cleanup method in itself, or, as we have seen, can be used in combination with skimming. ADAPTS, the Coast Guard's Air Deliverable Anti-Pol-

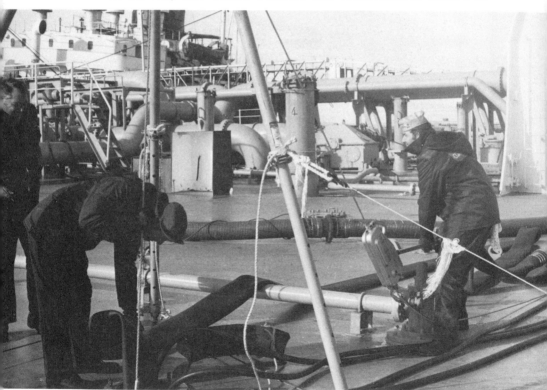

National Strike Force team using ADAPTS.

Sorbent pads and boom.

lution Transfer System, can pump oil at the rate of 1,800 gallons a minute into the hold of a waiting boat or floating storage tank. Elephantine vacuum pump trucks may be used to pump up spills close to shore. Oil that is pumped up can be stored and reused, thus pumping is a method of cleanup used whenever feasible.

Absorbents — sorbents, for short — soak up oil like a sponge. Sorbents are materials like straw, granular or matted polyurethane foam, cotton waste, shredded paper, or special chemicals like Sweden's bregoil herder. On land, the sorbents are raked and shoveled into the oil. On water, they may be mixed directly into the

Here a net suspended from a bridge is used as a boom to trap sorbents used to blot up a spill of about 8 million gallons of heavy oil stored in pools along the Schuylkill River (PA). The oil is kept in these pools until it is converted into tar, but a flood washed the oil over the retaining dikes.

Beach cleanup with sorbent boom and pads—very much a hands-on job.

**Snares or fibrous mops absorb oil on ice,
and then have to be picked up by pitchfork.**

oil, or they can also be made into pillows or pads, or packed into chicken wire to be used like dams or booms to catch oil as it moves downstream. Revolving belts of sorbent material may be used on skimmers. As they are driven through the spill, the belts pick up the oil, then are squeezed out into storage receptacles. Snares, or fibrous mops of sorbents, can absorb up to 40 times their weight in oil and are effective in cleaning up ice. Sorbents in large flat strips or bags of nylon mesh (for easy pickup later on) are used for beach cleanup. The sorbents are laid in trenches dug parallel to the waves. The

Here a machine made specially for cleaning beach sand of oil.

oil-water is washed onto the beach and into the trenches by wave action. The water percolates into the sand, leaving the oil in the sorbents.

The problem with sorbents is getting rid of them after they've done their job.

Burning is another way of cleaning up oil spills, but it is a method that usually can be used safely only on the open seas. The Swedish Coast Guard has used fire successfully to clean up spills in ice, and fire can be used if federal, state, and local fire prevention officials approve.

Getting the oil out of a wreck so it can be burned off is one big problem, as the *Torrey Canyon* demonstrated. The French have recently come up with something of a solution to this problem when they used hot water to force oil out of a tanker sunk in 300 feet of water.

Assuming that the oil is out, next comes the problem of getting a fire started, then of keeping it hot enough to continue burning in cold, splashing water. Special wicks like polyurethane foam are used to keep the fire going, and the oil is contained so that it will not cool too much by spreading too thinly. Light oils are less of a problem to burn, but light oils also evaporate faster and may not need to be burned at all.

Sinkage is a technique used in open seas only. Sinkage powders such as brick-dust or specially treated sand are poured over the oil to make it heavier so that it sinks to the sea bottom. This cleanup method requires official dispensation and sanction. Federal regulations forbid the additon of anything to the marine environment that might be more harmful than the oil being cleaned up. Since nothing is really known about the effects of sinkage on deepwater marine life, it is a cleanup method used with caution.

Microorganisms: A thought-provoking but not at present an important method of cleanup. The waters in which microorganisms can be used have to have oxygen, nitrogen, and phosphorus present in sufficient amounts to sustain them. Bacteria have been specially bred to ingest oil in a chronic oil-seep environment. A mix of these bacteria has been made into a commercial product for use in salt-water spills and another mix for those in fresh water is being developed.

Another experiment in using microorganisms to clean up spills has caused a front-page stir. On June 16,

1980, the United States Supreme Court in a landmark decision approved the issuance of a patent for a new life form created in the laboratory — a bacterium genetically engineered to digest oil spills. Bacteria that exist naturally can digest or degrade only one component of oil at a time; the genetically engineered bacterium can break down four.

The moral questions involved in genetic interference are complex, and bring the subject of cleaning up oil spills into the realm of the philosopher. The ecologist may also find genetically engineered or specially bred bacteria a problem: introducing new and oil-impregnated organisms in great numbers into an ecosystem does not seem to be an efficient way of keeping that system stable — one of the important goals of cleanup. And the effect on the food chain cannot even be guessed at.

Detergents: A more common but equally controversial method for spill cleanup involves detergents. The problems the British had with detergent cleanup of the *Torrey Canyon* spill — the extensive mousse formation, the chemically ravaged birds — remain a vivid memory. Surpisingly enough, the British still favor detergents, but the United States considers them only a cleanup method of last resort.

If you were to squirt some dishwashing liquid detergent into that oil slick you may have made earlier, you would see the oil dart away from the detergent. This is one of the complaints against detergents — if the oil darts away, it is harder to pick up and causes a problem over a wider area. However, the oil does move back together — slowly — since oil has a natural tendency to

A DC 4 "spray plane" sprays dispersant on an open-water spill.

do that. Now if you were to stir it vigorously, you would see the oil break up again, this time into thousands of tiny droplets. When surface-active detergents, *surfactants,* are used to clean up oil spills on our waterways, they are stirred into the oil and break it up into tiny bubbles in much the same way as in your cup. In time, these tiny bubbles of oil will oxidize and evaporate. The detergents are also *biodegraded,* broken down and ingested by bacteria, lichen, and fungi.

Contrary to U.S. government thinking, there are scientists and other experts who feel that today's improved biodegradable detergents, also called *dispersants,* are the best answer to cleaning up oil spills. They feel the United States should rethink its position on their use. Others are convinced that the spreading action of the detergents and the mousse formation are absolute contraindications to their use. Meanwhile, the On-Site Coordinator may authorize the use of rapid-acting dispersants only when the oil spill threatens human life, a large amount of animal life or breeding grounds, or presents a fire hazard. Detergents may also be used to avoid visible damage that may lead to economic, political, or environmental problems.

STORAGE AND DISPOSAL

Dispersants make mousse, sorbents make a mess. Mousse and mess must be disposed of — and oil, wherever possible, must be stored for re-refining. Oil picked up by skimmers or pumps can be stored in a variety of tanks, tank ships, tank trucks, inflatable tanks, portable tanks. Mousse will not yield up oil, but sorbents can, depending on the method used in their disposal.

The most effective way to dispose of sorbents is to dig a pit and place the sorbents on a platform within the pit. The oil is pressed out of the sorbents, drips into the pit, and then is pumped into tank trucks and returned to the refinery for reprocessing. A drawback to this type of pit disposal is that the weather has to be warm enough so the oil can drip freely. Then, of course, you still have to get rid of the sorbents.

Workers in the Santa Barbara spill, for instance, found themselves with 10,000 truckloads of oiled sorbents to be carted off and dumped.

Sorbents can sometimes be burned, but of course they are oily and thus smoky. There is the problem of heavy smoke polluting the air and possibly drifting over populated areas.

Another disposal method for the sorbents is *landspreading* — spreading the oiled debris over the ground

Storage bladder or tank, part of ADAPTS. Compressed to the size of an automobile for air drops, it expands to 140 feet.

and letting it rot. This method is widely used to dispose of refinery tank sludge. Oiled sand and gravel is sometimes spread on roads in the process of being built. The problem with landspreading is that oil can seep into groundwater, especially if done in the same area a number of times.

Probably the worst possible way of getting rid of oiled debris — sorbents or mousse — is to bury it. Yet the most widely used disposal method today is burial. Oil in the ground does not decompose. It can remain a

Smoke from one small section of burning sorbents.

Sorbents were burned in these drums, now being collected for scrap.

Most cleanup comes down to one person with a pitchfork or shovel and a strong back.

source of pollution for centuries, seeping into soil under cultivation and into groundwater.

Whatever the method of disposal chosen, it usually winds up a hands-on job, one person with a pitchfork or shovel against a mountain of mess.

LEAVING IT TO NATURE

There is one further consideration in cleaning up an oil spill, a most difficult one, and that is, *not* to clean it. Sometimes the best way to handle a spill is to do nothing, to let nature take care of it. Adding chemicals or bacteria or sinking powders, moving heavy equipment and hundreds of people into a sensitive area, may do more harm than is done by the oil. Cutting oiled plant life, a favored treatment, may not be wise. Left alone, the plants can act like a sponge to soak up the oil, thus preventing further danger to other elements of the environment. And if the plants are torn up, there can be no regrowth. Left alone, the roots may be able to re-establish themselves for regrowth. Most experts also feel that spills on the high seas do little harm to the oceans because the natural forces of evaporation, dilution, and decomposition will dispose of the oil. They point to the fact that during World War II twenty million barrels of oil were spilled in the submarine warfare off the Atlantic coast, with little permanent impact on the waters or the life in them.

In a sense, not doing anything can be the toughest approach of all. Nobody — not the environmentalists, not those who want to retrieve the oil, not the people who live in the area, not the oil companies who want to keep a good image — nobody is happy about doing nothing, except, perhaps, the keepers of the purse. But this does not mean one should lose sight of its validity in some cases. Action simply for the sake of action can be stupid, although it is hard not to be stampeded by demands of vociferous groups and the news media who may not understand the advisability of inaction. This is when the public relations member of the Spill Response Team assumes the most important role on that team!

9

Oil and the Quality of Life

An oil spill means more than wasted fuel, more than the many millions of dollars it may take for cleanup, more than an assault on our sensibilities, on our environment. An oil spill means loss of life — plant life, sea life, perhaps even human life. But perhaps the loss that disturbs the world most is among those most symbolic of life: the birds.

As early as 1922, oil-killed birds on her shores caused Great Britain to pass a law forbidding oil and waste dumping in her territorial waters. Then came the death of tens of thousands of birds from the *Torrey Canyon* spill, causing shock waves around the world. Despite heroic efforts day and night for months, the survival rate of those oiled birds was only one or two out of every hundred rescued.

A good deal of research into the care of oiled birds has gone on since then. But the survival rate today is not much better — perhaps four or five of every hundred birds that are brought for help. (That figure is higher

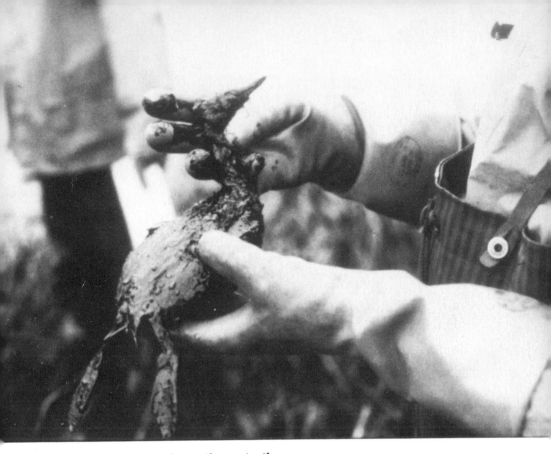

A grebe, covered with #6 (heavy) oil.

where selection of birds takes place before treatment and those with no chance of survival are left to die.)

A diving bird will die immediately of suffocation as it goes down into the oil. Swimming birds may be poisoned as they swallow the oil, which damages their kidneys and livers and causes internal bleeding. Birds whose feathers are oiled face a multitude of problems. Unlike human beings, birds have no mechanism inside their bodies to control their temperatures. Their feathers do this for them. The down that lies next to the bird's skin keeps air trapped against its body, preventing it from getting too hot or too cold. The trapped air also

Oiled birds, oiled beaches.

gives the bird buoyancy so it can float in water or rise in the air. To maintain that temperature and buoyancy, a bird's feathers must be clean and exactly arranged so they fit together. A bird keeps its feathers in order by *preening*, using its bill to comb and wax its feathers with a substance made in a gland under the tail. Oil makes the feathers gummy, and the bird cannot preen them apart. As it tries, its beak picks up more and more oil, which the bird swallows. The bird is poisoned or loses its buoyancy. Its body gets chilled if the air and water are cold, overheated if temperatures are hot and the sun is shining brightly. The bird dehydrates, losing body fluids essential to life. The chemicals in the oil burn and blister the bird's skin and its eyes. And it paddles off to die.

If oiled birds reach a source of expert help in time, some of the less badly oiled may be saved. Caring for birds is a hard, long, and dirty job, and the odds are against success. Strike teams do first aid but do not have sufficient resources in personnel or time to take on long-term responsibilities. Trained people and necessary facilities have to be set up at the time of the spill. There is only one permanent bird-cleaning station, the International Bird Rescue Research Center in Aquatic Park, Berkeley, California. Help usually comes from volunteer groups working under the federal Fish and Wildlife Service and the state wildlife conservation agency. These groups may be part of local birdwatching organizations including the Audubon Society, the SPCA, members of biology departments, nature clubs at local colleges and high schools, sportsmen's groups, various Scout organizations, and so on.

Anyone handling birds must have a permit from the government. This is not just red tape. It is required by a law meant to protect the birds and dates to the time when feathers were in high fashion, causing the wholesale slaughter of birds. Permits are rapidly available to responsible groups when there is an oil spill.

If you should find a bird that has been oiled and needs help, it is not practical — or good for the bird — to care for it yourself. Without a permit you are breaking the law. And, as much as you want to help, you probably cannot give an oiled bird the care it needs. Caring for an oiled bird requires knowledge and equipment most people do not have — and much patience and time. Seabirds make an incredible mess, and their care and feeding go on for 24 hours a day, possibly for weeks on end. And, heartbreakingly, no matter how much time you give, their chances of survival are very, very slim and grow slimmer with each passing day. As with any pet, losing a bird can be a very unhappy experience.

It is best for you and for the bird that it be brought to trained help: veterinarians, biologists, zoologists, ornithologists, and others with medical knowledge to give injections and medicines and physical treatment. You can find out where to go from the people in charge of the spill site or from the Coast Guard, EPA, the federal Fish and Wildlife Service or state wildlife agency in your area, or the SPCA. If there is a spill, temporary treatment facilities will be close to the site because fast first aid is essential to save the birds. Or an animal hospital may be used in an emergency.

You, as a volunteer, will be badly needed to do some of the thousand and one chores that are part of caring for birds oiled by a spill. The jobs won't be highly technical — more on the order of gathering newspapers to line the bottoms of pens and cleaning and sweeping the area. Volunteers are also needed to help with the all-important job of rounding up the birds to bring them in for treatment. This is done by moving on the birds carefully with large fishnets or by making a human chain. Birds will shy away, of course, and because it is important not to scare them anymore than they already are, volunteers should be trained in these techniques.

When it is a case of trying to keep the birds *away* from a slick, then the trick is to scare them as much as

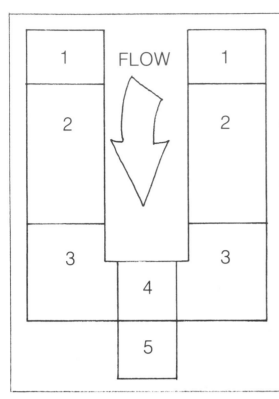

1. Reception: Identification of species; determination of potential for recovery; establishment of records; medication administration.
2. Washing & Cleaning: Locale for solvent baths, rinses, and pat-drying. Note: provide disposal facilities for used materials.
3. Boxing: Box assembly and placement of individual birds in completed boxes supplied with shredded paper floor.
4. Transporting: Caged birds sent to initial holding area for eight to ten hours; confirmation of records.
5. Holding Area: Indirect warming; food, and water supplied to caged birds.

Navy's schematic floor plan for bird-cleaning site.

possible. Volunteers in boats can patrol, wave flags, set off special alarms made for the purpose, shoot fireworks and propane exploders — making all the noise and movements they can to keep wildlife away.

Birds that are beached need to be handled gently, carefully, and speedily. First aid is given to remove oil from beaks and claws — and sometimes the handlers need first aid for scratches from beaks and claws: there's a knack to handling scared birds. Tranquilizers — for the birds — help. Covering the bird's head with a sock with a slit in the toe to accommodate its beak makes a good restrainer, keeps the bird warm, and somehow pacifies it.

Once the birds have been medically treated, they are cleaned. Some advise a rest period first, since the strain on the birds can kill them. Some experts, however, call for immediate cleanup.

There are a number of schools of thought on cleaning birds, each with advantages and disadvantages. They all agree, however, on the necessity for trained people to do the job.

Lightly oiled birds can be treated by having *fuller's earth* (a powder of absorbent clay) blown onto their feathers and then washed off. But most lightly oiled birds are able to fly and are not the ones usually brought to treatment centers.

Diagram of a Navy cleaning station arrangement.

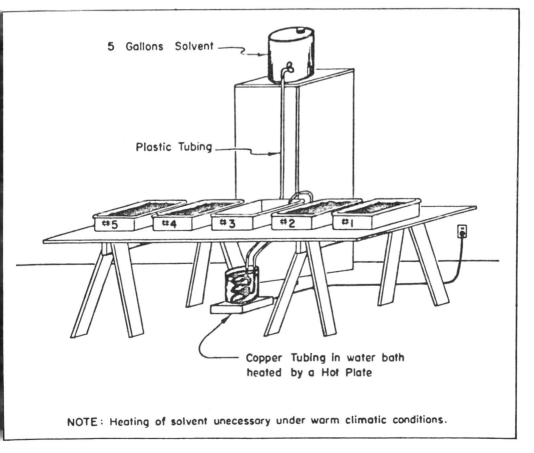

NOTE: Heating of solvent unecessary under warm climatic conditions.

For more heavily oiled birds, lard or cooking oils can be rubbed in and wiped off, but *only* in the direction in which the feathers lie. This method of cleaning is costly, and worse yet, very slow. The longer a wild bird is held in captivity, the less its chances for survival. For many, even a few days is too long.

Certain industrial *detergents* weakened with water work well on heavily oiled birds. You will remember that to work properly detergents have to be stirred up in oil. And there's the rub in *this* method — how to rub the detergent in without ruffling and damaging the birds' feathers. Slow patting or gentle stroking will do it, again only in the direction that the feathers lie. And again, this requires great patience and precious time. Detergents also need a tremendous amount of rinsing, or sores develop on the skin. Care has to be taken, also, that the birds' natural waxy substance with which they preen — their waterproofing — is not rinsed away with the detergents.

Solvents, liquids that can dissolve oil, do not need rinsing and work quickly. The fumes make the birds a little drunk, though, and their handlers slightly sick unless they wear respirators. But they sober up in a few hours — the birds do, anyway. The handlers just go on being sick. Another drawback to solvents is that they can injure the eyes, of both handlers and birds, should they splash or splatter. Solvents also have a very low flash point: at 107°F. they will go up in flames. This temperature is easily reached on a hot summer's day in some areas. Feathers are also more fragile after solvent use, and drying must be done with extra care.

Once the birds are past all this and safely dried

by heaters or gentle hand patting with towels or rags, they can be allowed to rest or sober up. Then they must be fed. Their diet varies according to their species. Mackerel, smelts, and minnows make the gulls, terns, herons, penguins, and loons happy. Insects, earthworms, and mealworms are fed to oyster catchers and phalaropes. And for ducks, geese, and swans there is a diet of grains, greens, and turkey pellets.

. Birds don't feed well in captivity. Sometimes they take food better if they are put into the water, and pools (usually of the backyard inflatable variety) must be provided for them. Sometimes, but only as a last resort, the food has to be forced through the bird's beak and down to its stomach by gently massaging the underside of its neck in a downward motion.

Pools are necessary, also, to give the birds the exercise they need. And when a bird can swim easily, it may be a sign that it's time for it to go back home, or to a similar habitat if the bird's home is still oiled. There is a difference of opinion among experts, however, as to whether a bird should be released at this time. Often, seemingly well birds die soon after being released from treatment centers, and some experts feel that birds should *molt*, lose their old feathers and grow new ones, before they are released. But this means keeping them in captivity for much longer periods of time, which other experts view as dangerous as early release.

There are experts, too, who feel that most — 95 percent — of the oiled birds that are rescued should be put quickly and painlessly to death. This would relieve the burden on crowded treatment facilities and allow overworked crews to concentrate on the birds that stand

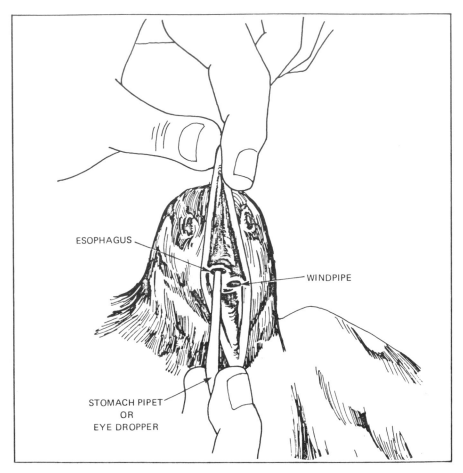

Feeding a bird is tricky. The food must go down the esophagus, the passage to the stomach. If food goes into the windpipe, the bird will suffocate.

the best chance of survival or are members of an endangered species.

Concerned groups of animal lovers, humane societies, wildlife and conservation agencies, zoological societies, are encouraging research on ways to help oiled wildlife. These groups are also trying to prepare for emergencies so that treatment centers can be set up with minimum delay and staffed with trained people from the area who would work with spill response teams. The International Bird Rescue Center in Berkeley, for instance, offers courses on a contractual basis to interested groups. But it is difficult for private groups to move about the country, and it is virtually impossible for their members to give the amount of time — often weeks — necessary to the job. This would seem to be a problem best handled by a government strike force of trained, mobile staff and equipment. Such a group could go wherever there is a spill, would have the latest and best equipment and techniques, and would be able to give the 24-hour care necessary, drawing on local groups for assistance. The possibility of government funds being allocated to a mobile bird rescue team is slim — very slim indeed — with today's tight budgets, so for the moment we are in the realm of pure theory.

Money is a problem — or, rather, the lack of money. Funds for bird care, protected breeding, research projects, etcetera, are not high on the list of priorities when money is tight. Cleanup and compensation funds adminstered by state and federal agencies are built primarily from taxes on barrels of oil shipped and on fines. Insurance funds are increasing premiums. The companies who pay these taxes and fines and insurance premiums do not absorb them. They pass them on to the consumer, who pays them at the gas pump, in heating bills, and in the bills for hundreds of products most of us don't even know are connected to petroleum at all.

You and your family are paying for cleaning up oil spills. What is the cost to you of cleaning up that swamp, that wild bird?

At the same time, there is an increased awareness of the responsibility of the spiller to pay not only for cleaning up oil spills but for the loss to humankind of natural resources, losses that have to be computed in dollars and cents. A Federal Appeals Court has said,

> In recent times, mankind has become increasingly aware that the planet's resources are finite and that portions of the land and sea which at first glance seem useless often contribute in subtle but critical ways to the environment capable of supporting both human life and other forms of life on which we all depend.

The case being ruled on involved a tanker spill of 1.5 million gallons of crude oil in a Puerto Rican mangrove swamp. Cleanup costs had already been recovered from the spiller, who had also paid claims of local fishermen and owners of a nearby salt pond and hotel. But Puerto Rico had claimed damages of $14.7 million on behalf of the Puerto Rican citizens for the ruin of the mangrove swamp. Puerto Rico had been awarded $5.5 million — far above the market value of the swamp. The spiller appealed, but the Appeals Court affirmed the right of the public to compensation for a natural resource most of them had never seen but whose value to humanity could not be denied . . . although the Court questioned the value of that amount in hard cash.

Again what is the value to the world of a swamp? A bird? And how do you translate that value into currency? And from whom does that money ultimately come?

116

CHAPTER

10

Working Today for Tomorrow

The research, the experiments continue worldwide on the effects of petroleum spills on plant and animal life in an ecosystem. And the search for more and better solutions to the problems of prevention and cleanup of oil spills receives unabated attention.

Researchers are developing new booming techniques: chemicals that can be sprayed on shorelines without harming the life there, and bubble barriers that are inexpensive enough and easy enough to install to be widely practical. Chemical sorbents and herders that can be reused or burned as fuel when cleanup is over, and skimmers that work more efficiently in fast currents and high waves, are some other goals of research.

To test new products, methods, and equipment, there is the Naval Construction Battalion Center in California, and researchers around the world come to the EPA spill research center at Edison, New Jersey. Here a tank 667 feet long, 66 feet wide, and 11 feet deep provides a safe place for testing oil-spill cleanup. The

Mass culture chambers used to test oil-exposed lobster larvae.

OHMSETT tank.

tank has a name almost as long as it is wide: Oil and Hazardous Materials Simulated Environmental Test Tank, or OHMSETT.

OHMSETT has a wave-maker at one end that ruffles the water into waves up to two feet high. At the other end of the tank is a kind of beach to absorb the waves. OHMSETT can be filled with fresh or salt water,

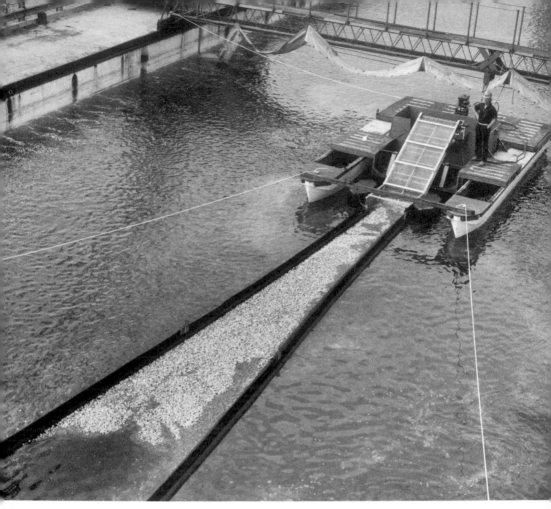

Sorbent harvester power unit mounted on catamaran being tested in OHMSETT tank.

and it even has machinery for simulating currents. A movable bridge tows test equipment through the water and also contains oil tanks to spread a slick. OHMSETT has the convenience of bubblers along the sides to keep the oil off walls. No cleanup necessary here, and therefore no loss of time and no extra expense.

Most of the equipment tested at OHMSETT is developed by private firms with financial help from the federal government. These firms hope to attract potential users and win lucrative contracts. Evaluators from the EPA study performances and make recommendations. This kind of testing is also an opportunity for teaching and learning more about spills.

To this end, also, the Coast Guard is engaged in an ambitious project of documentation. Records are kept of everything that happens in a spill, everything that is done, in order to learn from every spill — not to speak of the need for documentation for future legal claims. All reported spills are also recorded into a computer in the hope that someday enough information will be accumulated to make spill prevention possible. The computer would tell where, and under what weather conditions, and what time of day a spill would most likely occur. Contingency plans could be laid more efficiently and more effective precautions taken at this most dangerous time and place. Contingency planning is growing more sophisticated and effective as conflicting plans are being reconciled and more is learned about spills.

Scientists are particularly concerned about safeguarding the Artic from the effects of possible spills. Oil spills in those icy waters are virtually uncleanable with today's technology, and while spills left to nature will decompose, that decomposition is much slower in extreme cold. A spill in Arctic ice may take ten years or so to decompose. A very large oil spill contaminating a very wide area of polar ice could disturb the weather patterns of the world. If pack ice, the ice that covers the oceans extending out from the Poles, is blackened by oil, it would not reflect the sun's light and the weather would grow colder. At the same time, the blackened ice would absorb more of the sun's heat and therefore melt, flooding the oceans — and the shorelines and the cities along those shorelines. Such a catastrophe would involve oil spills in amounts that are inconceivable to us today, but not perhaps to the world of tomorrow.

In the sub-Antarctic waters of Chile, in a remote area not far from Cape Horn, scientists are studying the effects of a large spill from the supertanker *Metula*. The *Metula* went aground on August 9, 1974, the dead of winter in that southern hemisphere. She spilled almost 52,000 tons of light crude oil and 2,000 tons of heavy bunker oil. Because of the remoteness of the area, the extreme cold and winds, and the few hours of daylight in which to work, cleanup was left to nature. Scientists, therefore, have been able to use the site as a valuable laboratory in which to study how an ecosystem in an extremely cold climate recovers from a major oil spill.

The site of the spill from the *Amoco Cadiz* has also proven valuable for research, albeit not of icy waters. A marine laboratory has been operating in that region of Brittany for over a century, so scientists have unusually complete information about the area before the spill for comparative studies, as well as the facilities to undertake long-term research.

Turning spills into constructive learning experiences is one step — a giant one — toward finding the answers to our questions about oil on our troubled waters. However, these projects cost a great deal of money — and most countries' economies are as troubled as their waters. A three-year study of the Ixtoc I spill proposed by a group of federal agencies was not funded,

The VLCC *Metula* being offloaded by an Argentine tanker. The *Metula* ran aground one mile offshore of Barranca Pt., Strait of Magellan, polluting some 40 miles of Chilean shoreline. The site became a laboratory.

so we have lost an important opportunity to learn more about oil in our marine environment. As government spending decreases, private groups may be able to take up the slack, although many researchers are partially supported by government grants, and so their efforts, too, may be limited. And no private group can do the jobs of the Coast Guard and EPA, whose budgets are going down to the point where curtailment of important preventive programs may result.

Ironically, the very effectiveness of spill preven-

123

tion and cleanup programs is curtailing funding: public interest in oil on our troubled waters is lessened as the problem lessens. When there are no huge headlines about spills, public outcry diminishes, Congressional outlays cease. Yet even in years like 1980, when the amount of oil spilled was statistically less then half of previous years, a lot of oil entered the world's waters. Statistics gathered by the Center for Short-Lived Phenomena, a private group monitoring the volume of oil spillage in waters worldwide, show spills of 149 million gallons of oil from 199 accidents, a further unknown amount from 83 more accidents, and at least 100 million gallons more from incidents in the war between Iran and Iraq. Four hundred eighty people were killed or reported missing and over one hundred fifty were injured in blowouts, refinery explosions, tanker accidents, and other spill-related incidents. Some 100,000 birds were killed. . . .

We cannot afford that loss to life, that loss of oil. Whatever the cost to the pocketbook of programs of prevention, detection, and cleanup, it seems small enough to pay when the quality of life — indeed, life itself — is at stake.

INDEX